HEATHCLIFF

THE BIG SPORT

by  Geo Gately

TOR

A TOM DOHERTY ASSOCIATES BOOK
NEW YORK

This is a work of fiction. All the characters and events portrayed in this book are fictitious, and any resemblance to real people or events is purely coincidental.

HEATHCLIFF©: THE BIG SPORT

Originally published by Marvel Comics in magazine form as portions of HEATHCLIFF #2, #7, #23, #25, #27, #28; HEATHCLIFF'S FUNHOUSE #2, #5

A Tor Book
Published by Tom Doherty Associates, Inc.
49 West 24th Street
New York, N.Y. 10010

ISBN: 0-812-51087-9

First printing: February 1991

Printed in the United States of America

0 9 8 7 6 5 4 3 2 1

ACKNOWLEDGMENTS

Take Meow to the Ball Game—*Angelo DeCesare, writer, Warren Kremer, penciler, Jacqueline Roettcher, inker*

The Runaway Trainer—*Angelo DeCesare, writer, Warren Kremer, penciler, Roberta Edelman, inker*

Touchdown Tabby—*Dave Manak, writer, Warren Kremer, penciler, Ruth Leon, inker*

Ghost in the Outfield—*Michael Gallagher, writer, Warren Kremer, penciler, Jacqueline Roettcher, inker.*

Horse Feathers—*Michael Gallagher, writer, Warren Kremer, penciler, Jacqueline Roettcher, inker*

At the Rat—*Michael Gallagher, writer/penciler, Jacqueline Roettcher, inker*

He's into Video Games—*Angelo DeCesare, writer, Warren Kremer, penciler, Ruth Leon, inker*

A Giant of a Time—*Michael Gallagher, writer, Milton Knight, penciler, Jacqueline Roettcher, inker*

Teamwork—*Angelo DeCesare, writer, Warren Kremer, penciler, Roberta Edelman, inker*

Alley Cat—*Angelo DeCesare, writer, Ben Brown, penciler, Jacqueline Roettcher, inker*

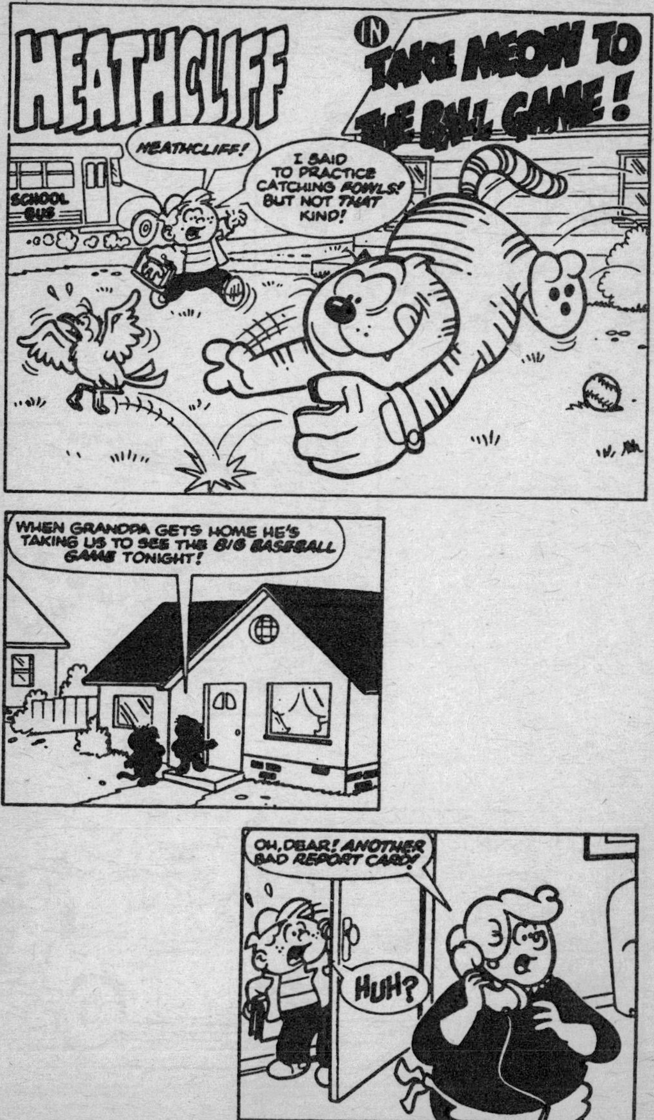
HEATHCLIFF
IN
TAKE MEOW TO THE BALL GAME!
SCHOOL BUS
HEATHCLIFF!
I SAID TO PRACTICE CATCHING FOWLS! BUT NOT THAT KIND!
WHEN GRANDPA GETS HOME HE'S TAKING US TO SEE THE BIG BASEBALL GAME TONIGHT!
OH, DEAR! ANOTHER BAD REPORT CARD!
HUH?

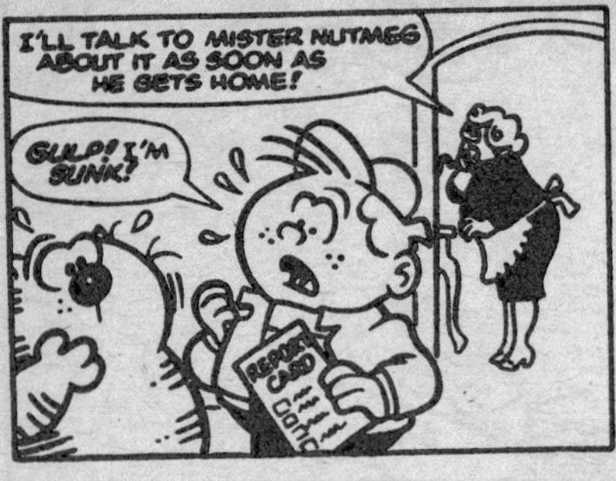
I'LL TALK TO MISTER NUTMEG ABOUT IT AS SOON AS HE GETS HOME!
GULP! I'M SUNK!
REPORT CARD

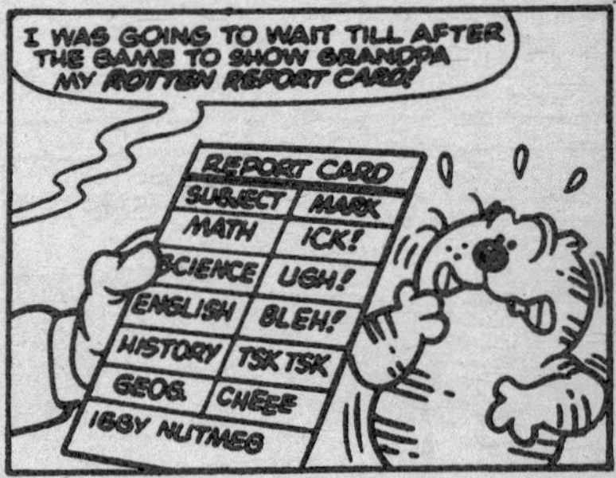
I WAS GOING TO WAIT TILL AFTER THE GAME TO SHOW GRANDPA MY ROTTEN REPORT CARD!
REPORT CARD
SUBJECT MARK
MATH ICK!
SCIENCE UGH!
ENGLISH BLEH!
HISTORY TSK TSK
GEOG. CHEEE
IGGY NUTMEG

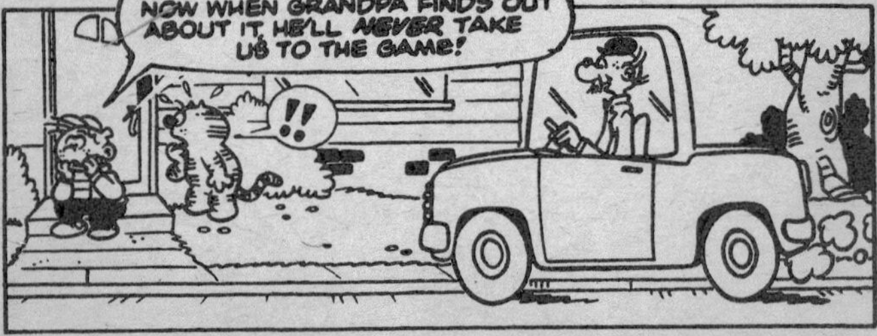
NOW WHEN GRANDPA FINDS OUT ABOUT IT, HE'LL NEVER TAKE US TO THE GAME!
!!

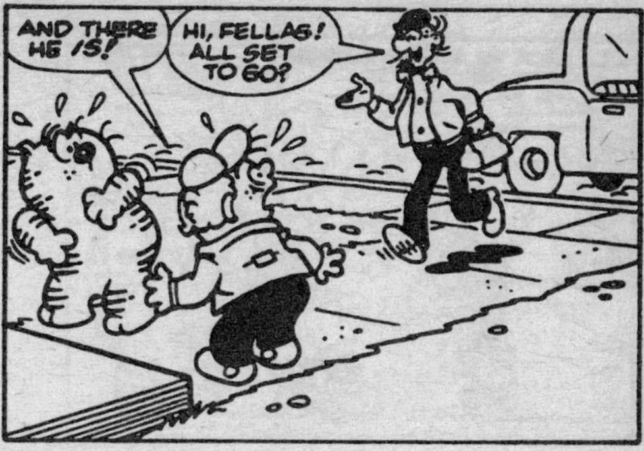
AND THERE HE IS!
HI, FELLAS! ALL SET TO GO?

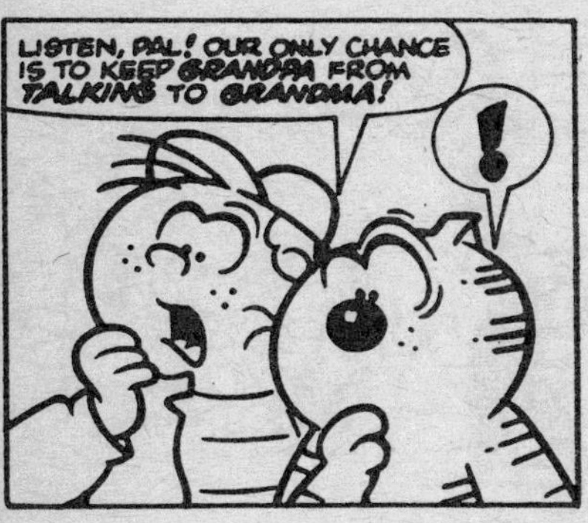
LISTEN, PAL! OUR ONLY CHANCE IS TO KEEP GRANDPA FROM TALKING TO GRANDMA!
!

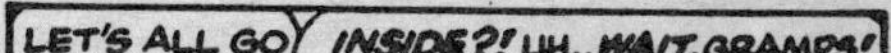
LET'S ALL GO INSIDE!
INSIDE?! UH...WAIT, GRAMPS! HEATHCLIFF HAS SOMETHING IMPORTANT TO SHOW YOU!

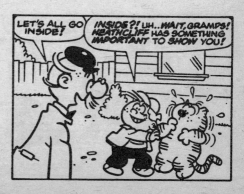

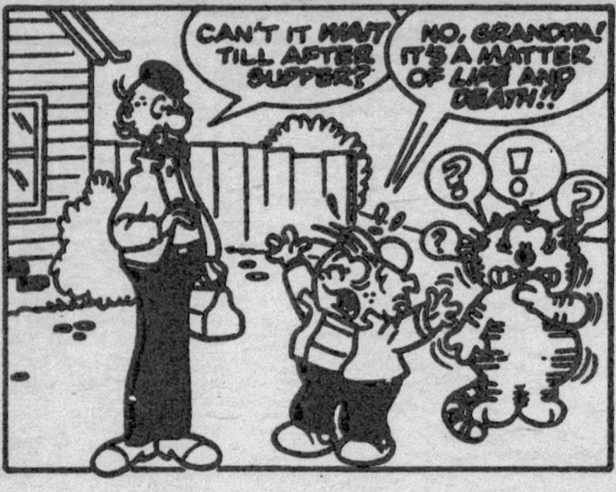
CAN'T IT WAIT TILL AFTER SUPPER?
NO, GRANDPA! IT'S A MATTER OF LIFE AND DEATH!!
?
!
?
?

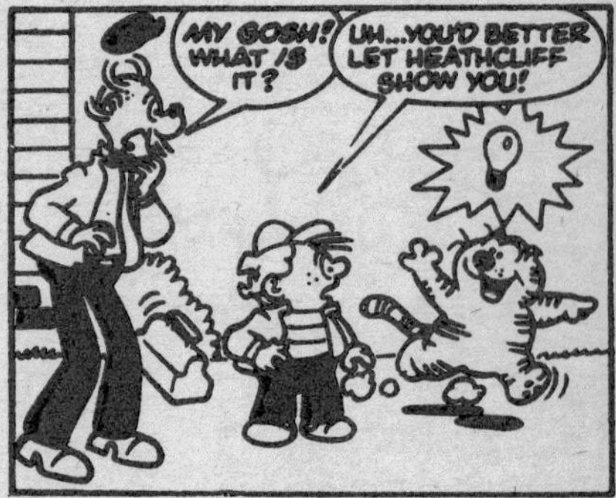
MY GOSH! WHAT IS IT?
UH...YOU'D BETTER LET HEATHCLIFF SHOW YOU!

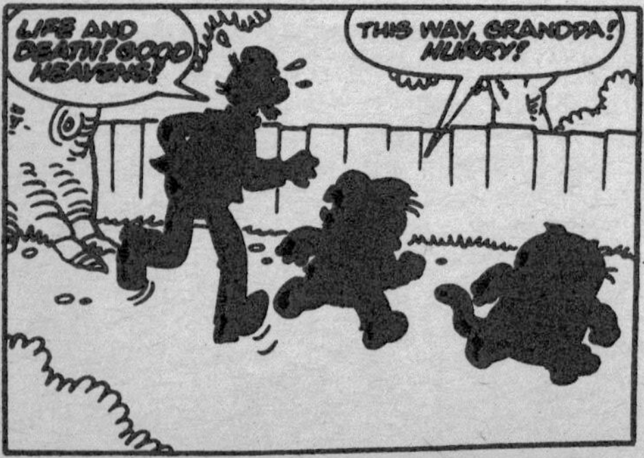
LIFE AND DEATH! GOOD HEAVENS!
THIS WAY, GRANDPA! HURRY!

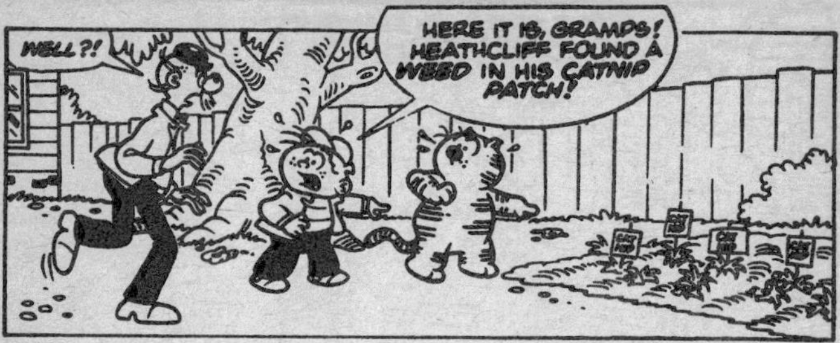
WELL?!
HERE IT IS, GRAMPS! HEATHCLIFF FOUND A WEED IN HIS CATNIP PATCH!

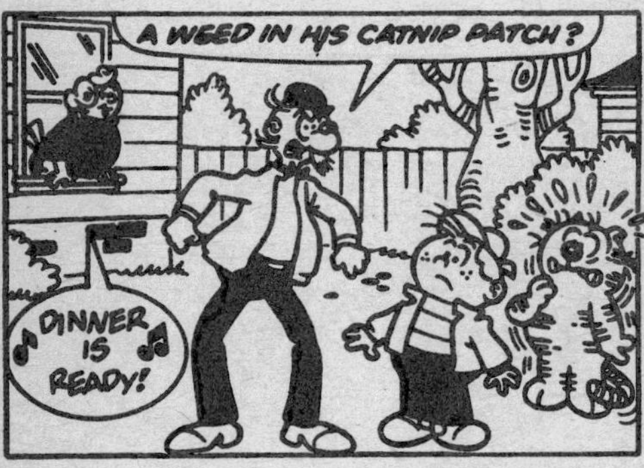
A WEED IN HIS CATNIP PATCH?
DINNER IS READY!

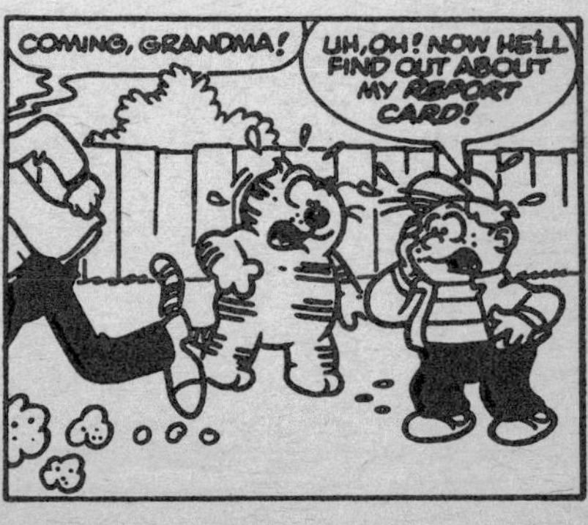
COMING, GRANDMA!
UH, OH! NOW HE'LL FIND OUT ABOUT MY REPORT CARD!

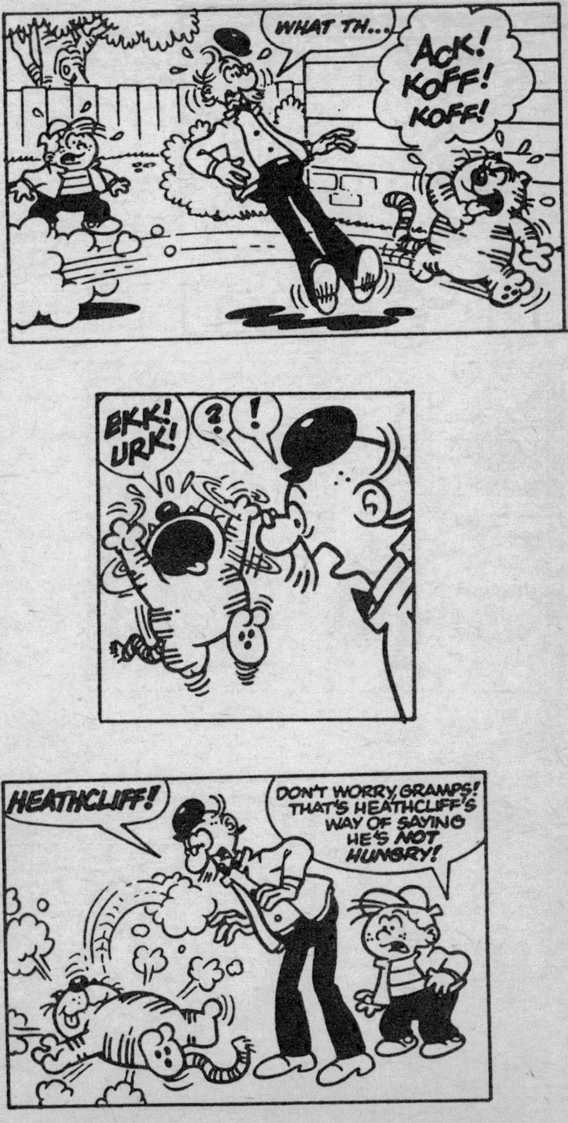
WHAT TH...
ACK! KOFF! KOFF!
EKK! URK!
?
!
HEATHCLIFF!
DON'T WORRY, GRAMPS! THAT'S HEATHCLIFF'S WAY OF SAYING HE'S NOT HUNGRY!

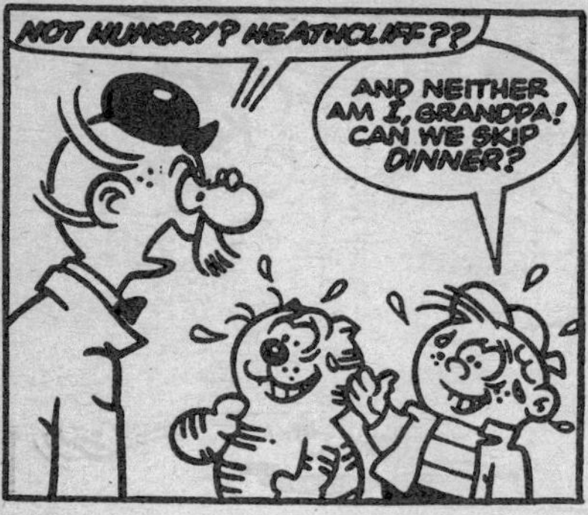
NOT HUNGRY? HEATHCLIFF??
AND NEITHER AM I, GRANDPA! CAN WE SKIP DINNER?

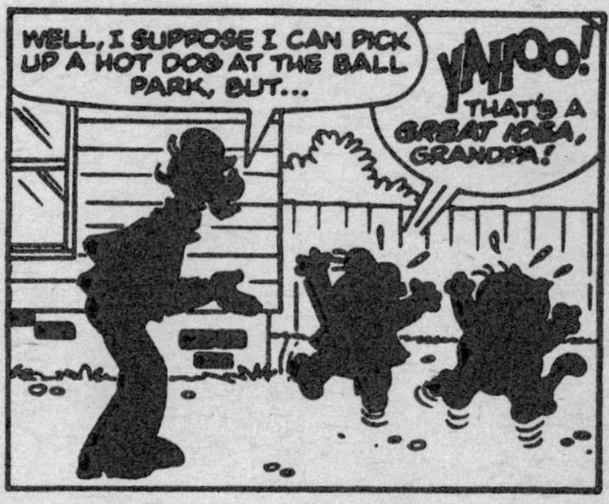
WELL, I SUPPOSE I CAN PICK UP A HOT DOG AT THE BALL PARK, BUT...
YAHOO! THAT'S A GREAT IDEA, GRANDPA!

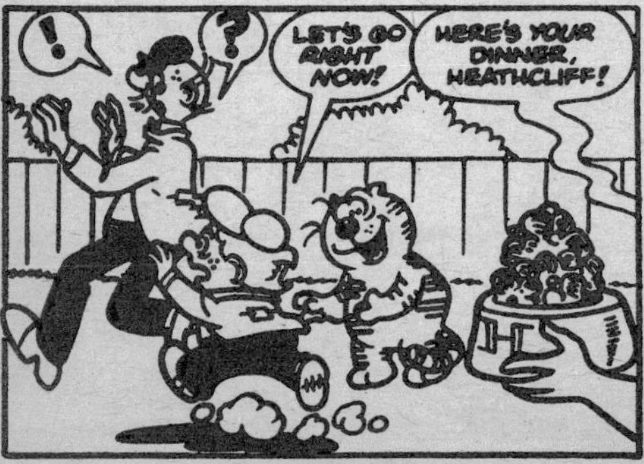
!
?
LET'S GO RIGHT NOW!
HERE'S YOUR DINNER, HEATHCLIFF!

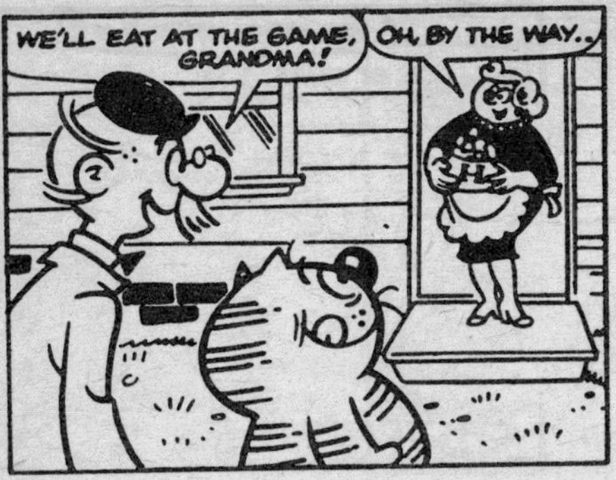
WE'LL EAT AT THE GAME, GRANDMA!
OH, BY THE WAY...

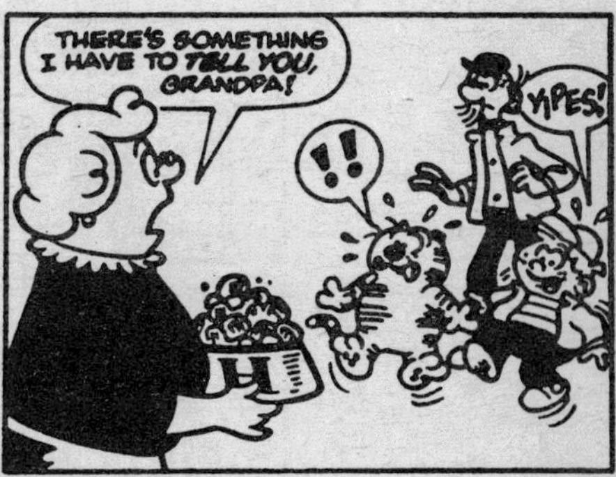
THERE'S SOMETHING I HAVE TO TELL YOU, GRANDPA!
!!
YIPES!

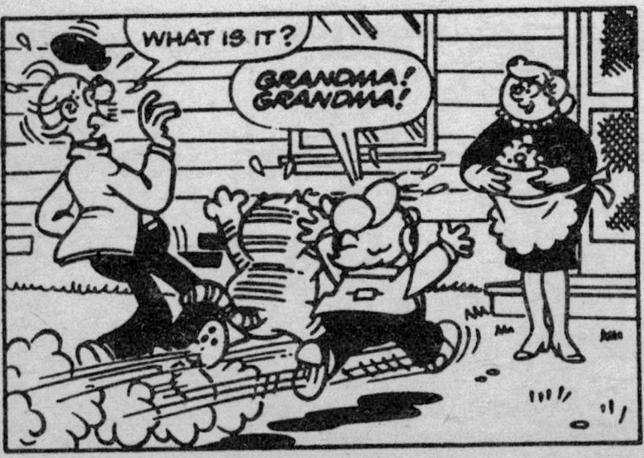
WHAT IS IT?
GRANDMA! GRANDMA!

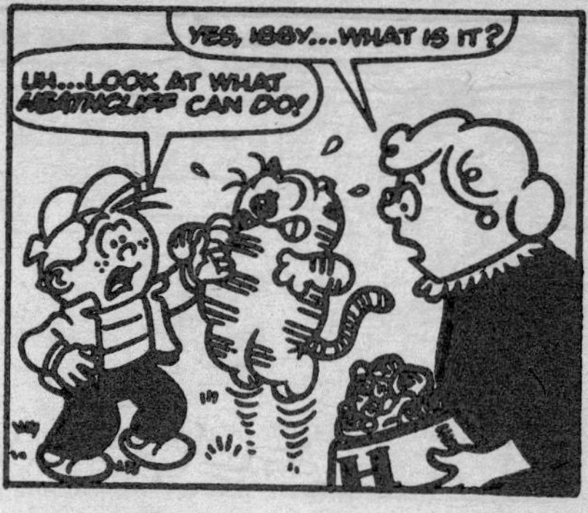
UH...LOOK AT WHAT HEATHCLIFF CAN DO!
YES, IGGY...WHAT IS IT?

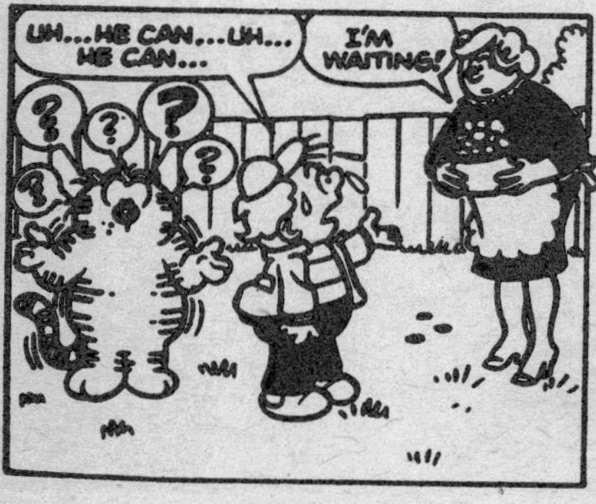
UH...HE CAN...UH...
HE CAN...
I'M WAITING!

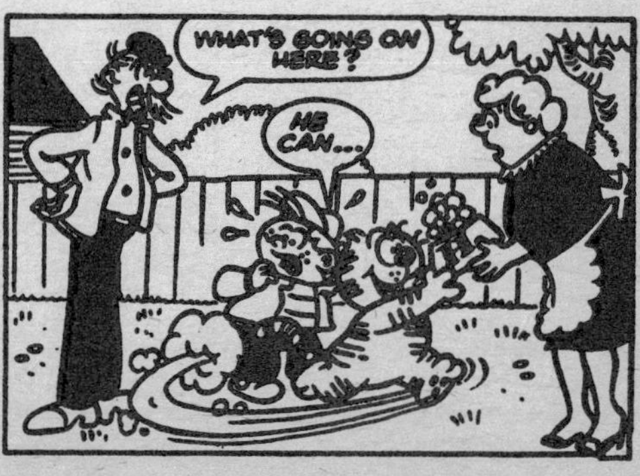
WHAT'S GOING ON HERE?
HE CAN...

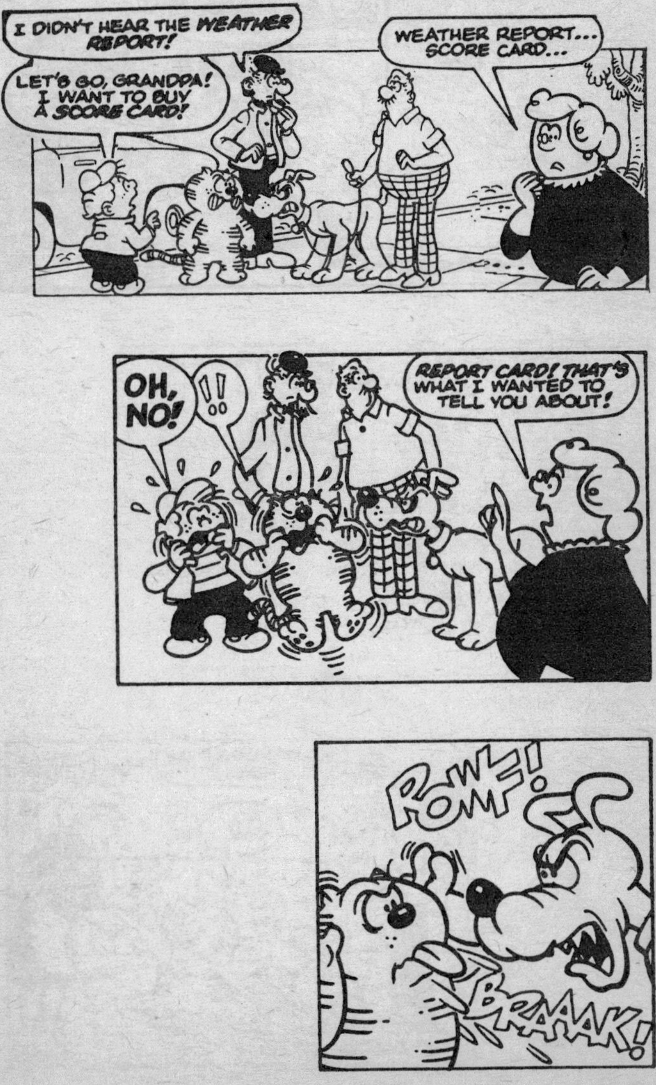
I DIDN'T HEAR THE WEATHER REPORT!
LET'S GO, GRANDPA! I WANT TO BUY A SCORE CARD!
WEATHER REPORT... SCORE CARD...
OH, NO!
!!
REPORT CARD! THAT'S WHAT I WANTED TO TELL YOU ABOUT!
ROWF!
BRAAAK!

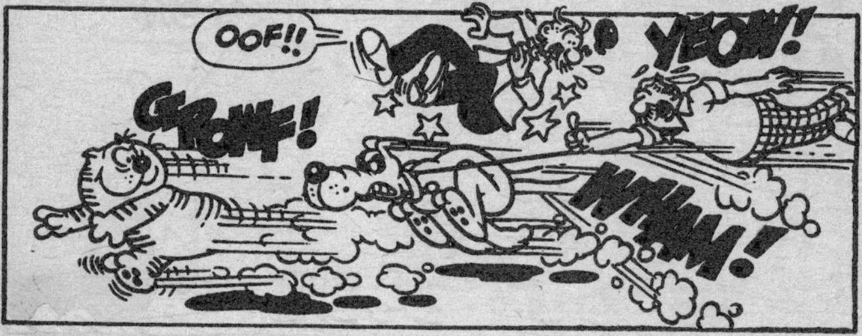
OOF!!
YEOW!
GROWF!
WHAM!

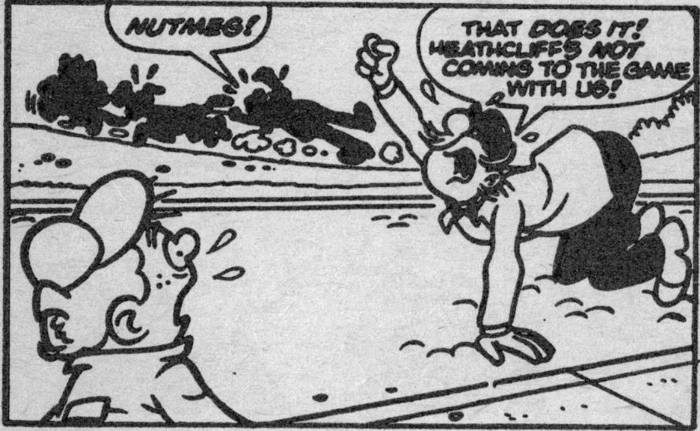
NUTMEG!
THAT DOES IT! HEATHCLIFF'S NOT COMING TO THE GAME WITH US!

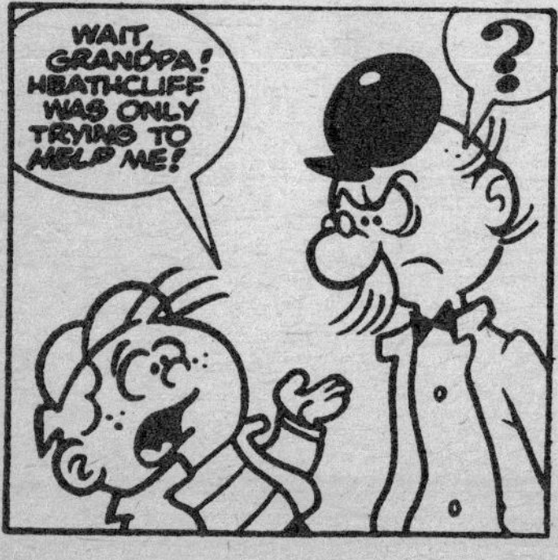
WAIT, GRANDPA! HEATHCLIFF WAS ONLY TRYING TO HELP ME!
?

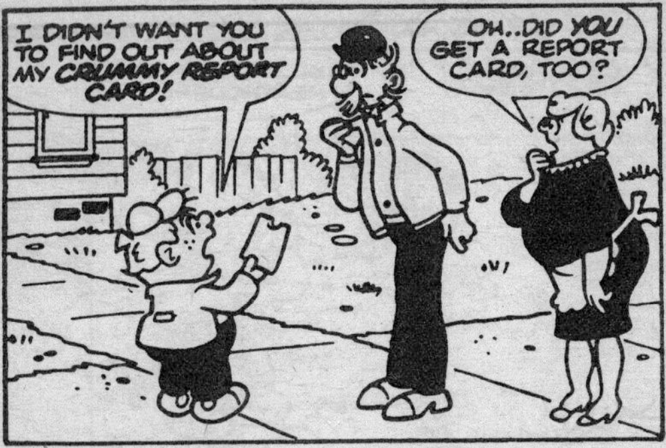
I DIDN'T WANT YOU TO FIND OUT ABOUT MY CRUMMY REPORT CARD!
OH..DID YOU GET A REPORT CARD, TOO?

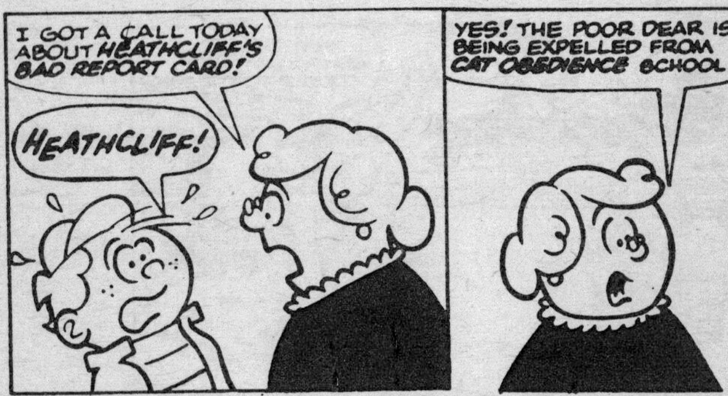
I GOT A CALL TODAY ABOUT HEATHCLIFF'S BAD REPORT CARD!
HEATHCLIFF!
YES! THE POOR DEAR IS BEING EXPELLED FROM CAT OBEDIENCE SCHOOL!

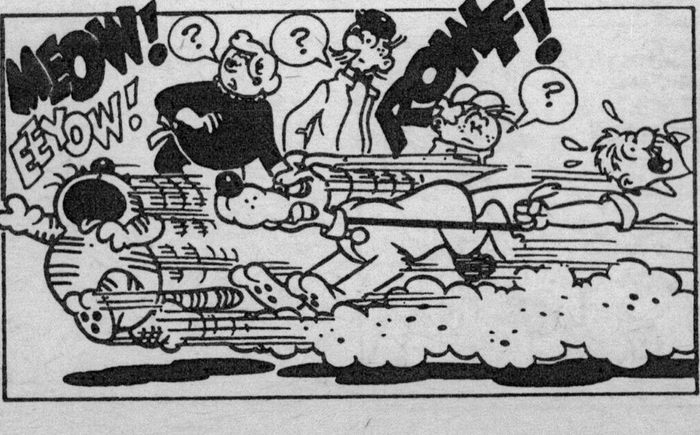
MEOW!
EEYOW!
?
?
POW!
?

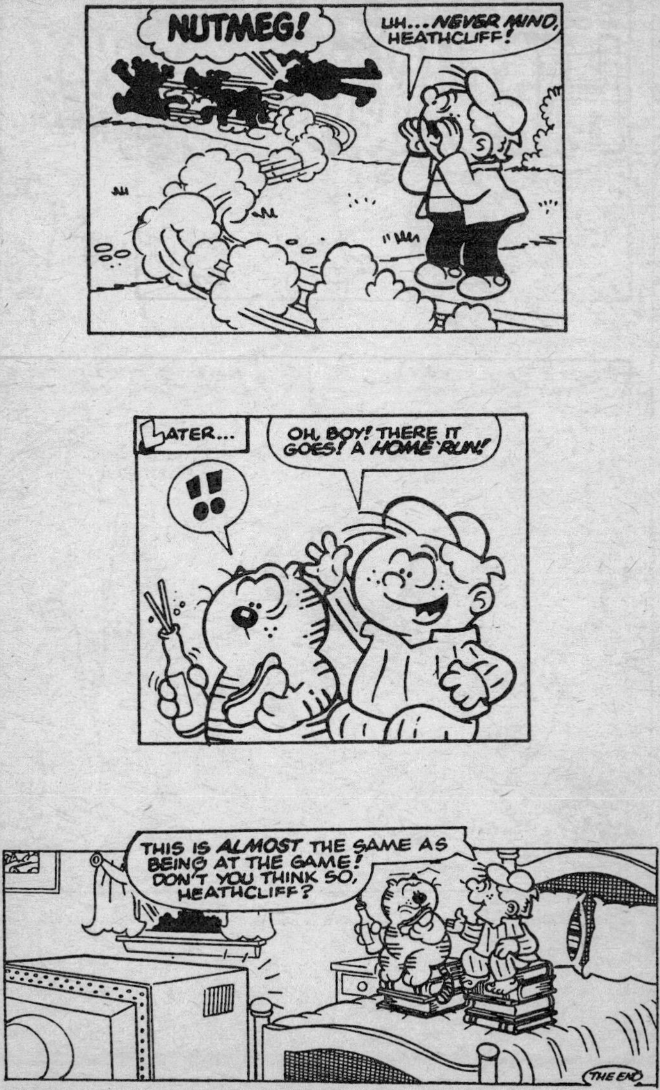
NUTMEG!
UH... NEVER MIND, HEATHCLIFF!
LATER...
OH, BOY! THERE IT GOES! A HOME RUN!
!!
THIS IS ALMOST THE SAME AS BEING AT THE GAME! DON'T YOU THINK SO, HEATHCLIFF?
THE END

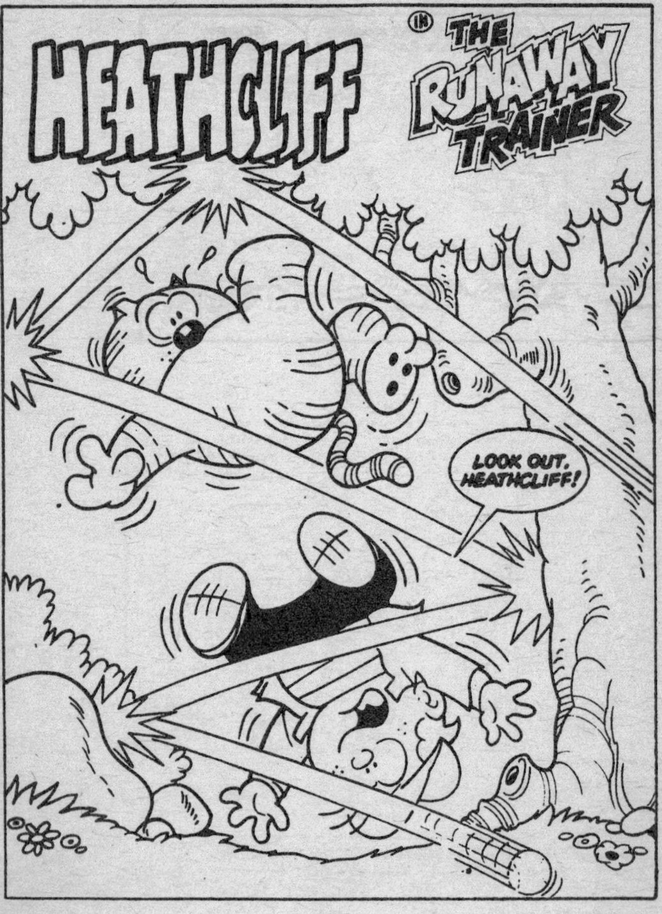
HEATHCLIFF
IN
THE RUNAWAY TRAINER
LOOK OUT, HEATHCLIFF!

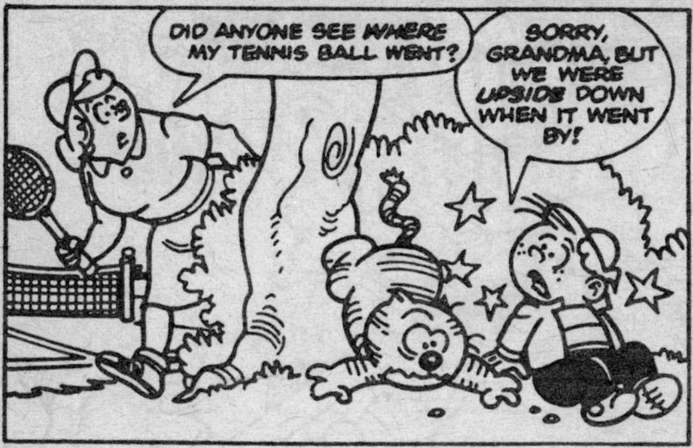
DID ANYONE SEE WHERE MY TENNIS BALL WENT?
SORRY, GRANDMA, BUT WE WERE UPSIDE DOWN WHEN IT WENT BY!

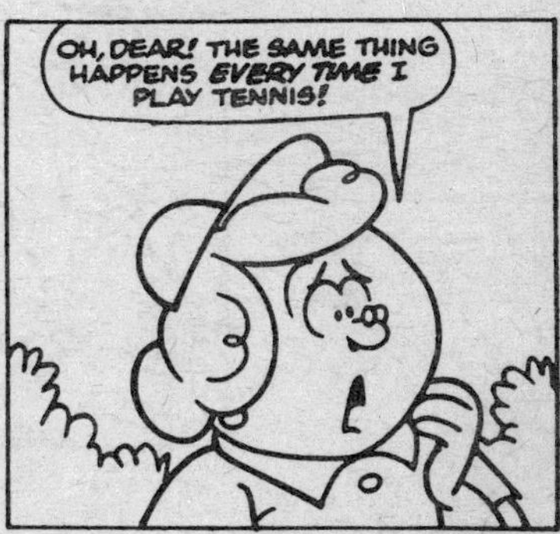
OH, DEAR! THE SAME THING HAPPENS EVERY TIME I PLAY TENNIS!

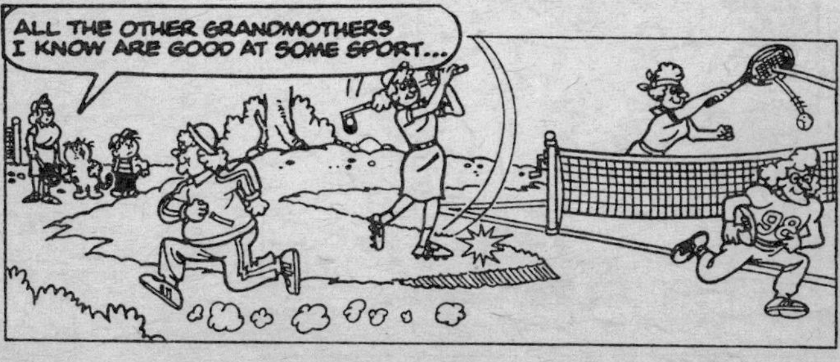
ALL THE OTHER GRANDMOTHERS I KNOW ARE GOOD AT SOME SPORT...

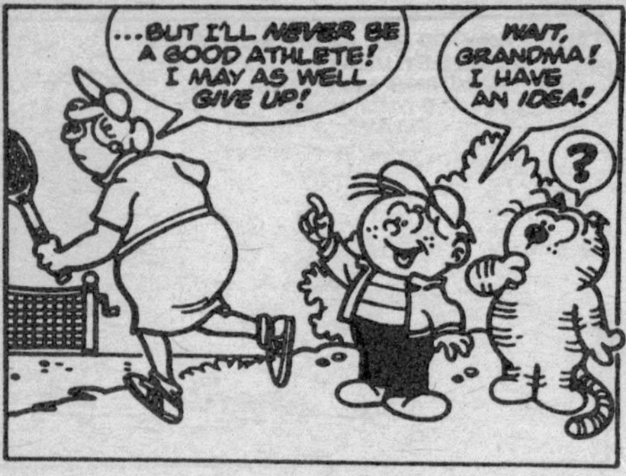
...BUT I'LL NEVER BE A GOOD ATHLETE! I MAY AS WELL GIVE UP!
WAIT, GRANDMA! I HAVE AN IDEA!
?

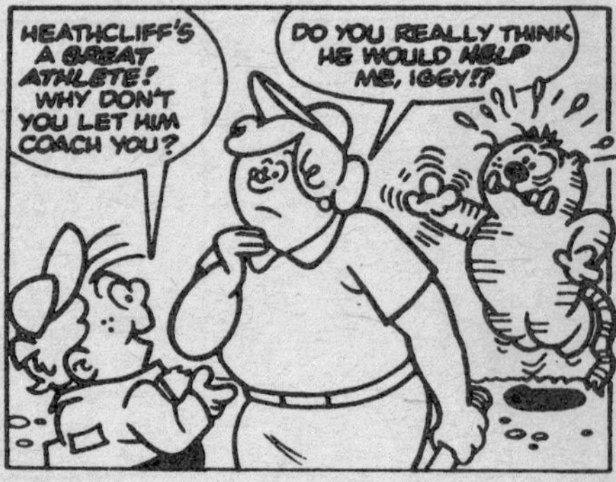
HEATHCLIFF'S A GREAT ATHLETE! WHY DON'T YOU LET HIM COACH YOU?
DO YOU REALLY THINK HE WOULD HELP ME, IGGY!?

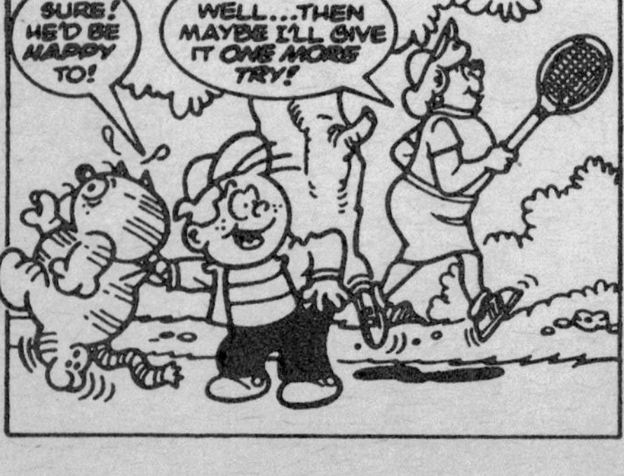
SURE! HE'D BE HAPPY TO!
WELL...THEN MAYBE I'LL GIVE IT ONE MORE TRY!

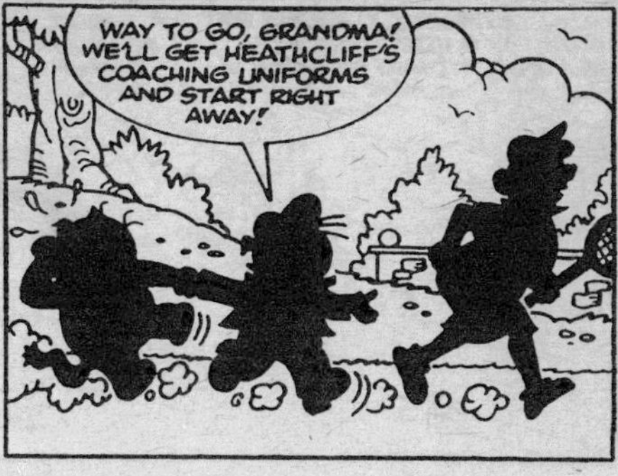
WAY TO GO, GRANDMA! WE'LL GET HEATHCLIFF'S COACHING UNIFORMS AND START RIGHT AWAY!

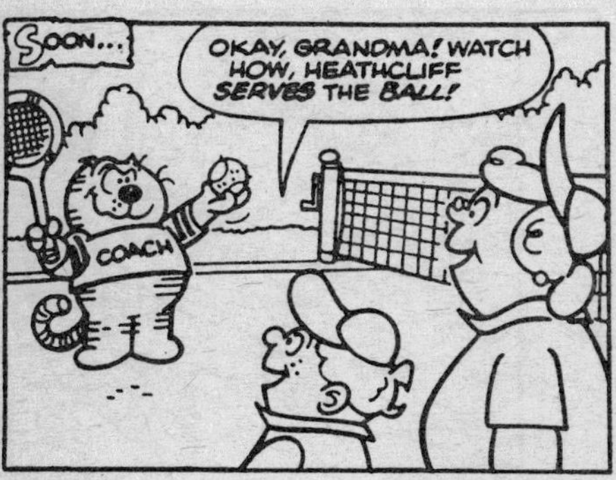
SOON...
OKAY, GRANDMA! WATCH HOW, HEATHCLIFF SERVES THE BALL!
COACH

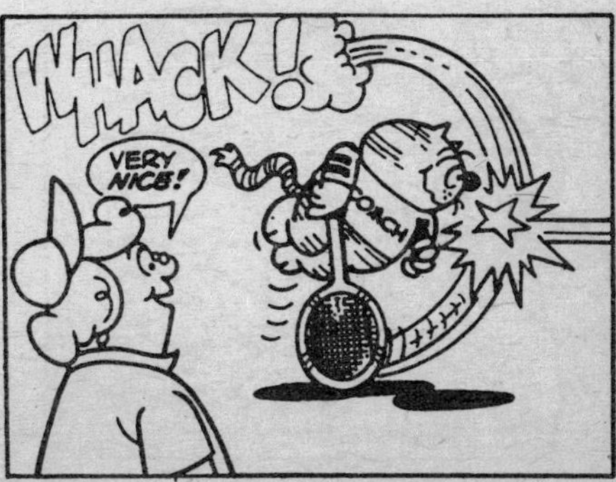
WHACK!
VERY NICE!
COACH

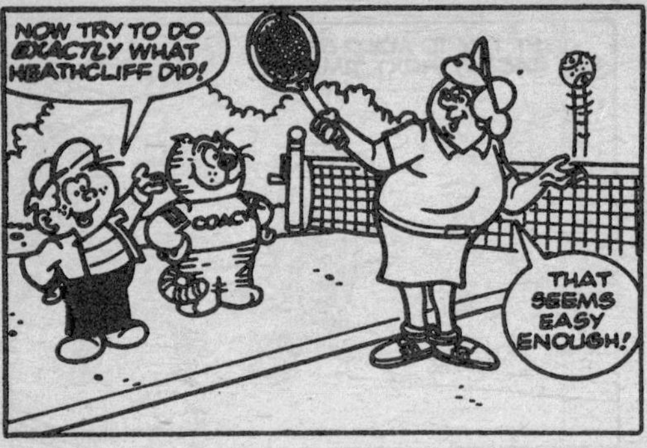
NOW TRY TO DO EXACTLY WHAT HEATHCLIFF DID!
COACH
THAT SEEMS EASY ENOUGH!

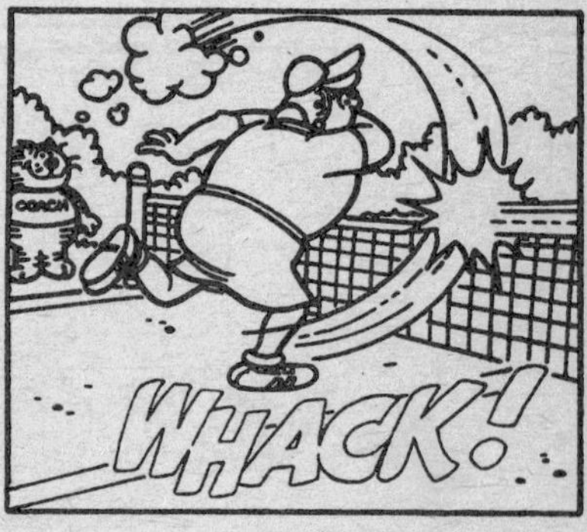
COACH
WHACK!

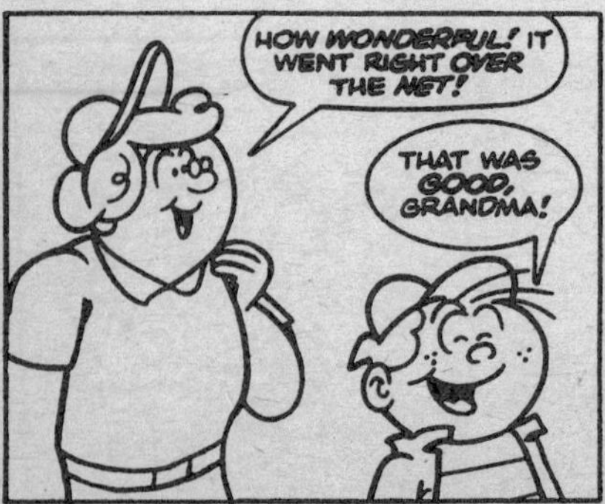
HOW WONDERFUL! IT WENT RIGHT OVER THE NET!
THAT WAS GOOD, GRANDMA!

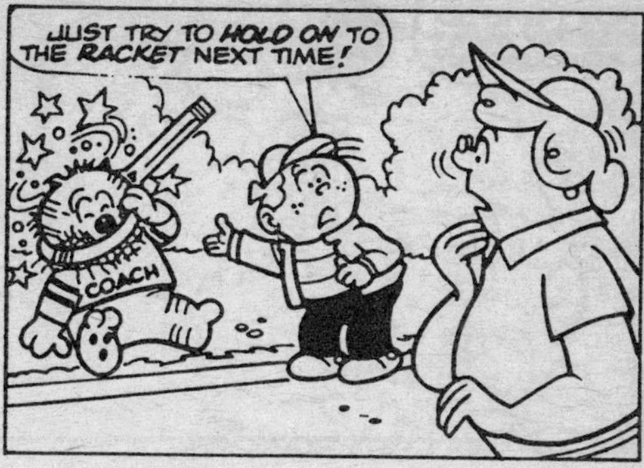
JUST TRY TO HOLD ON TO THE RACKET NEXT TIME!
COACH

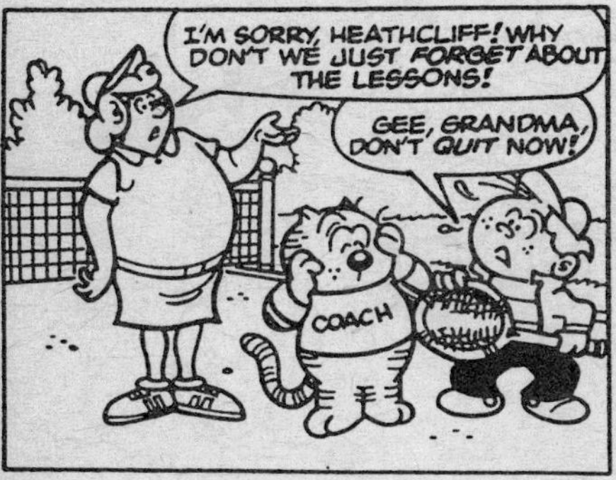
I'M SORRY, HEATHCLIFF! WHY DON'T WE JUST FORGET ABOUT THE LESSONS!
GEE, GRANDMA, DON'T QUIT NOW!
COACH

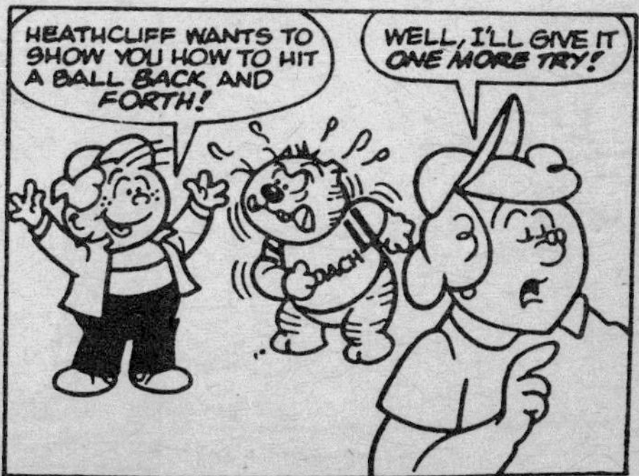
HEATHCLIFF WANTS TO SHOW YOU HOW TO HIT A BALL BACK AND FORTH!
WELL, I'LL GIVE IT ONE MORE TRY!
COACH

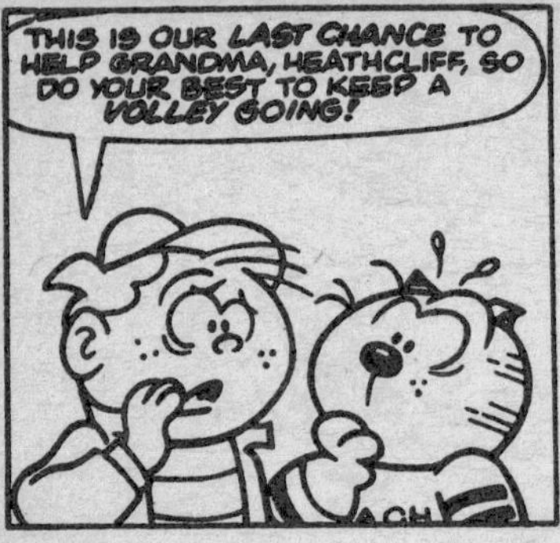
THIS IS OUR LAST CHANCE TO HELP GRANDMA, HEATHCLIFF, SO DO YOUR BEST TO KEEP A VOLLEY GOING!

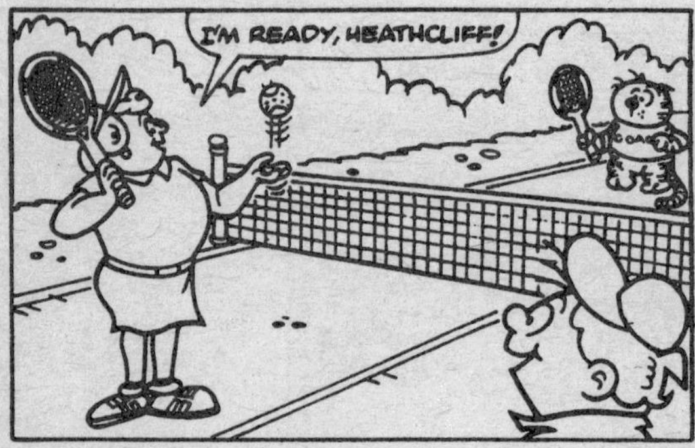
I'M READY, HEATHCLIFF!

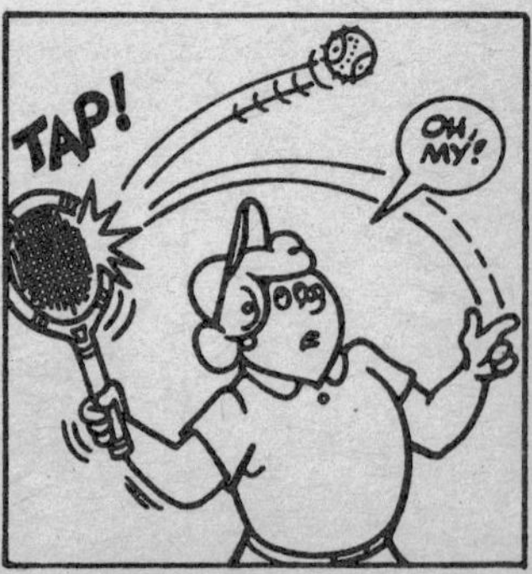
TAP!
OH, MY!

I'M AFRAID I DIDN'T HIT IT VERY HARD!
DON'T WORRY, GRANDMA! HEATHCLIFF WILL GET IT!
WAY TO GO, PAL!
SPROING!
UH, OH!

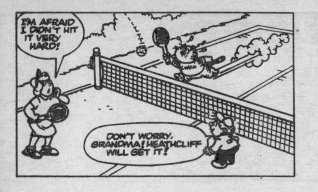

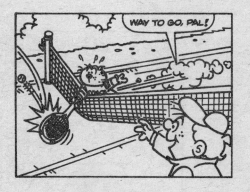

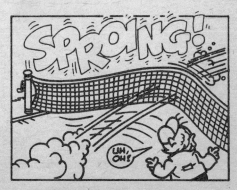

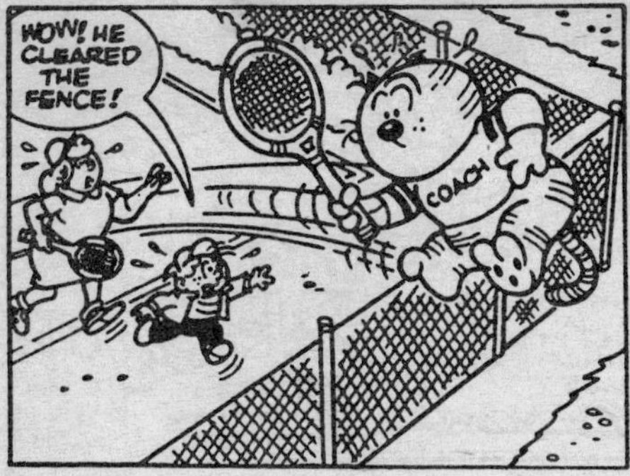
WOW! HE CLEARED THE FENCE!
COACH

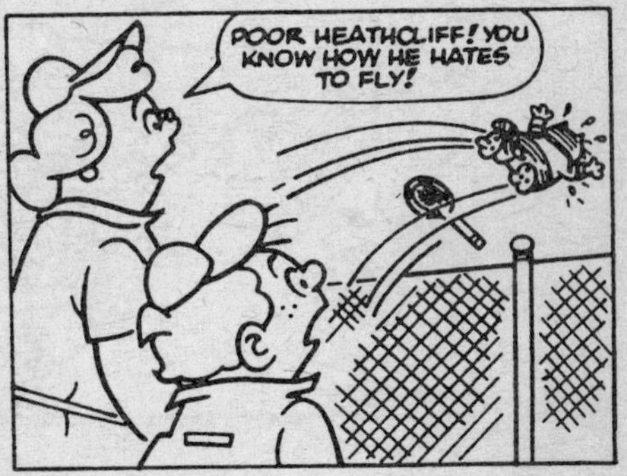
POOR HEATHCLIFF! YOU KNOW HOW HE HATES TO FLY!

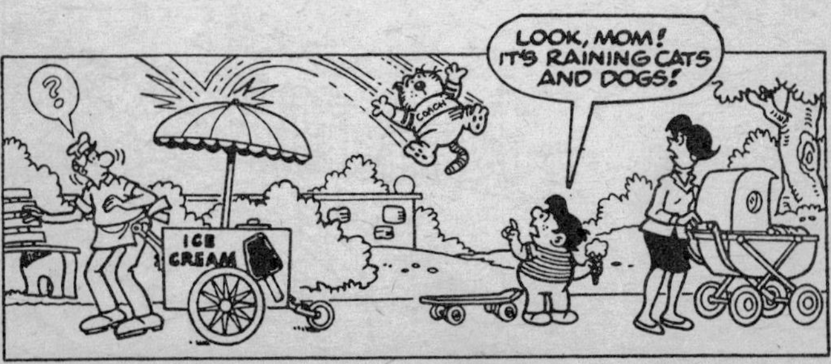
?
ICE CREAM
COACH
LOOK, MOM! IT'S RAINING CATS AND DOGS!

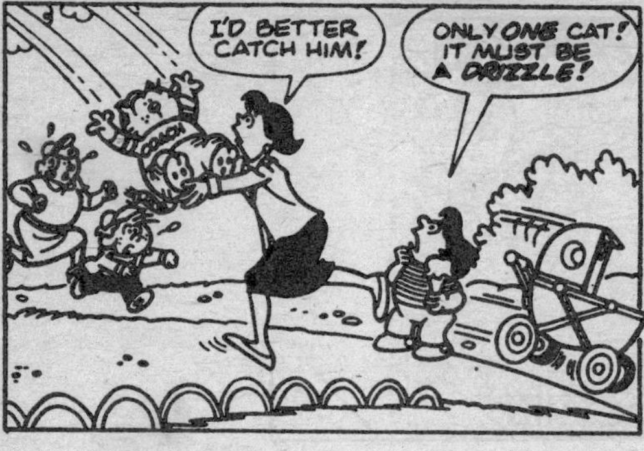
I'D BETTER CATCH HIM!
ONLY ONE CAT! IT MUST BE A DRIZZLE!
COACH

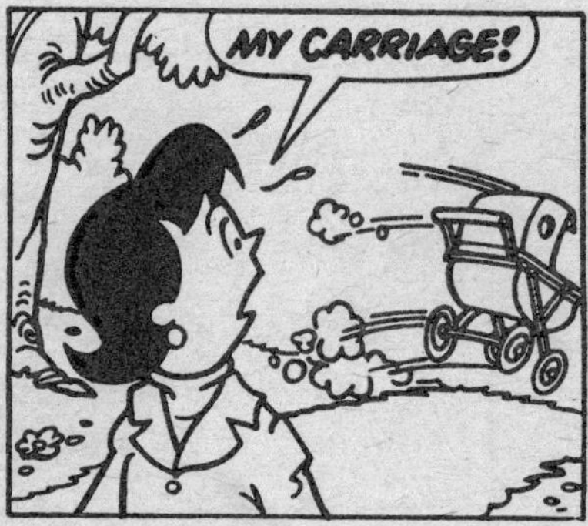
MY CARRIAGE!

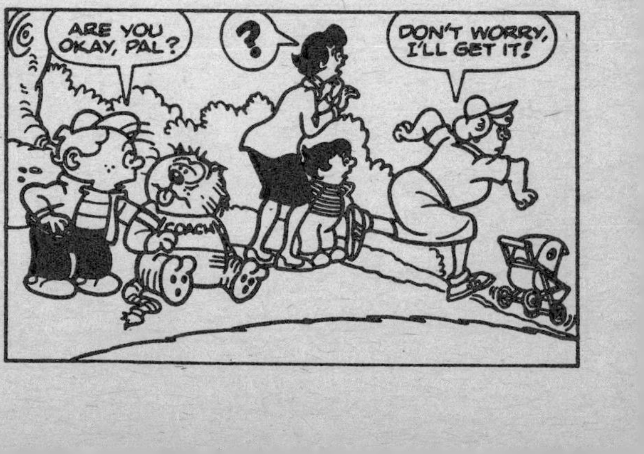
ARE YOU OKAY, PAL?
?
DON'T WORRY, I'LL GET IT!
COACH

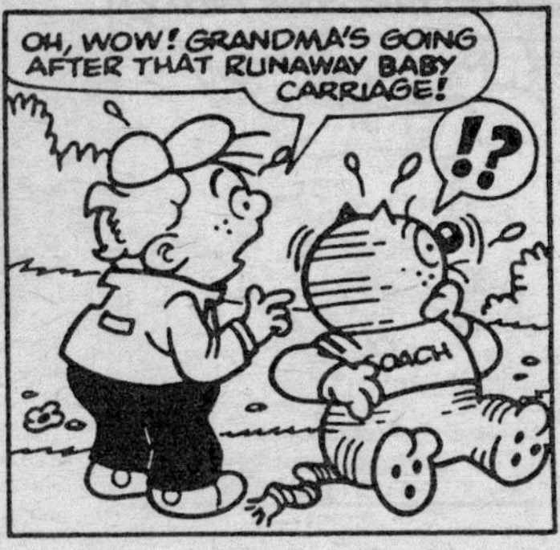
OH, WOW! GRANDMA'S GOING AFTER THAT RUNAWAY BABY CARRIAGE!
!?
COACH

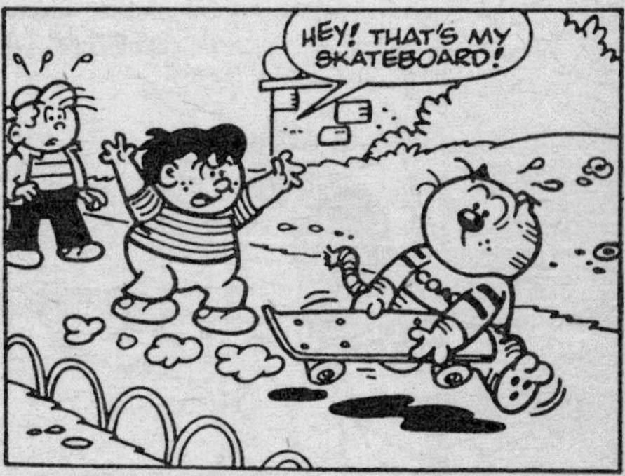
HEY! THAT'S MY SKATEBOARD!

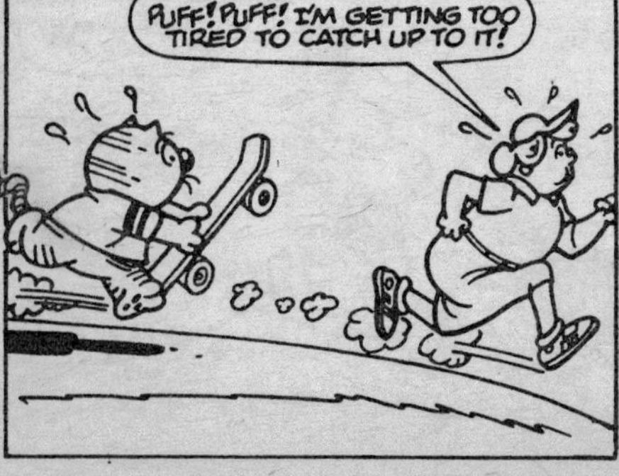
PUFF! PUFF! I'M GETTING TOO TIRED TO CATCH UP TO IT!

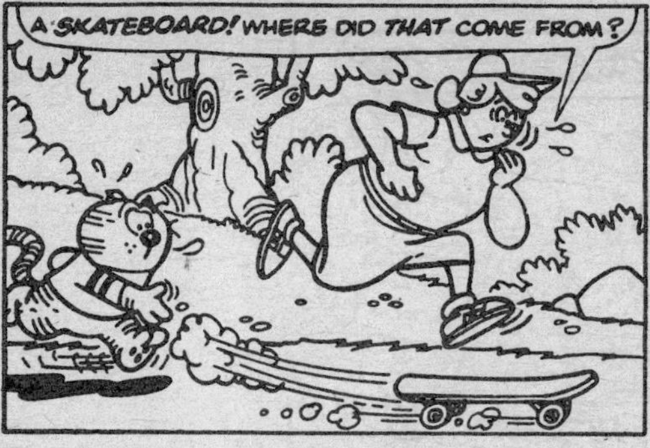
A SKATEBOARD! WHERE DID THAT COME FROM?

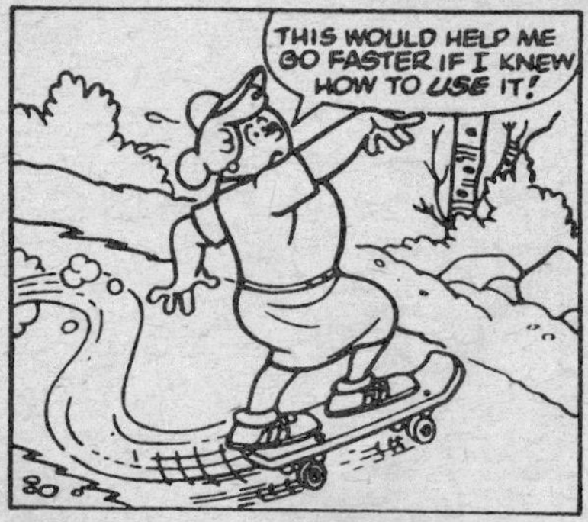
THIS WOULD HELP ME GO FASTER IF I KNEW HOW TO USE IT!

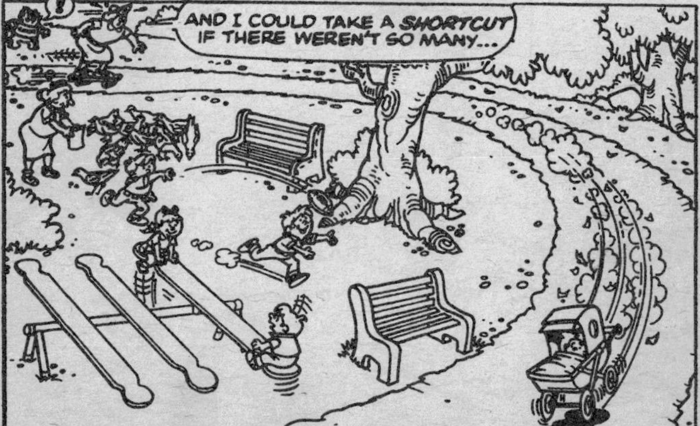
AND I COULD TAKE A SHORTCUT IF THERE WEREN'T SO MANY...

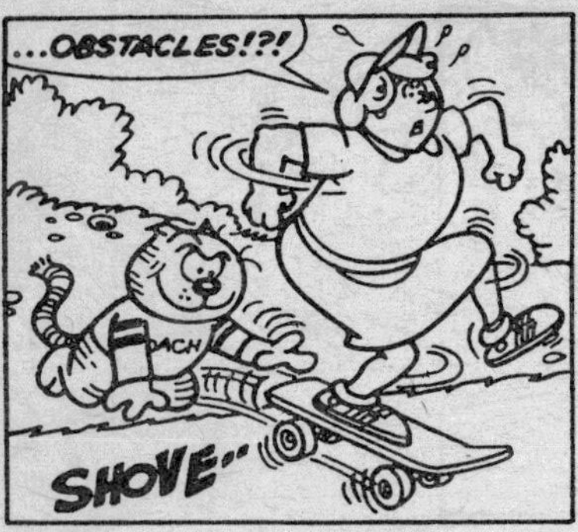
...OBSTACLES!?!
COACH
SHOVE..

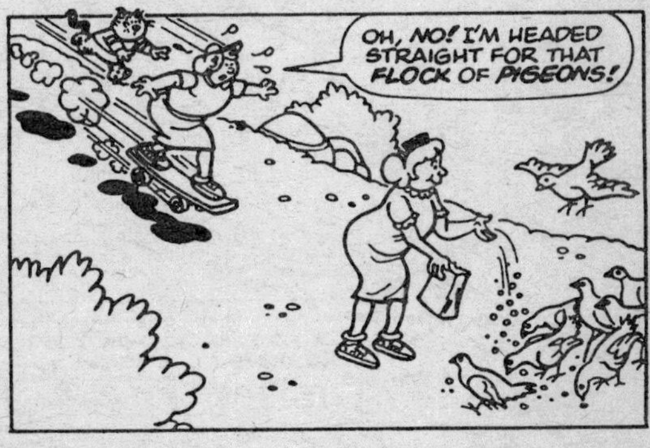
OH, NO! I'M HEADED STRAIGHT FOR THAT FLOCK OF PIGEONS!

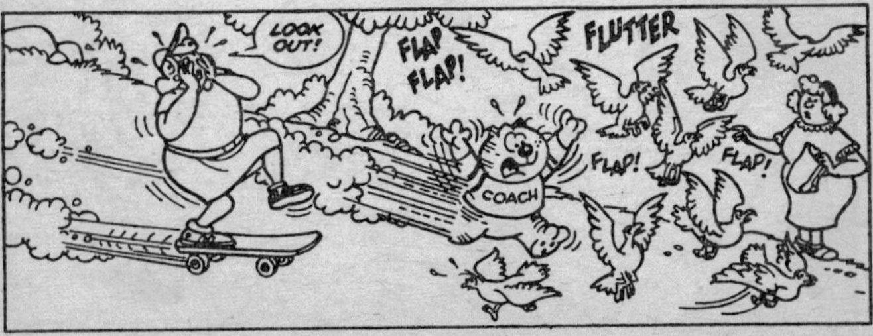
LOOK OUT!
FLAP FLAP!
FLUTTER
COACH
FLAP!
FLAP!

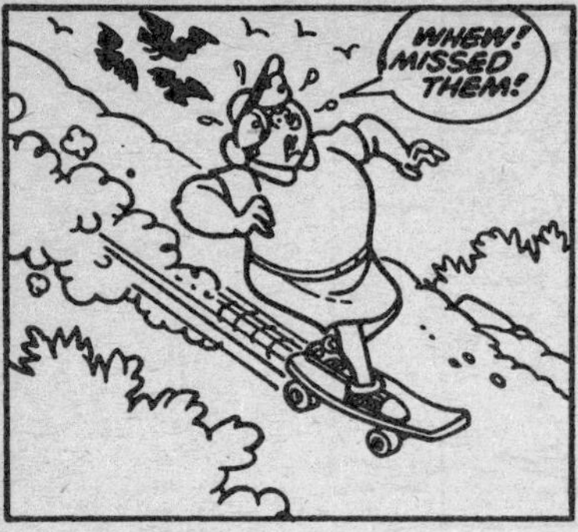
WHEW! MISSED THEM!

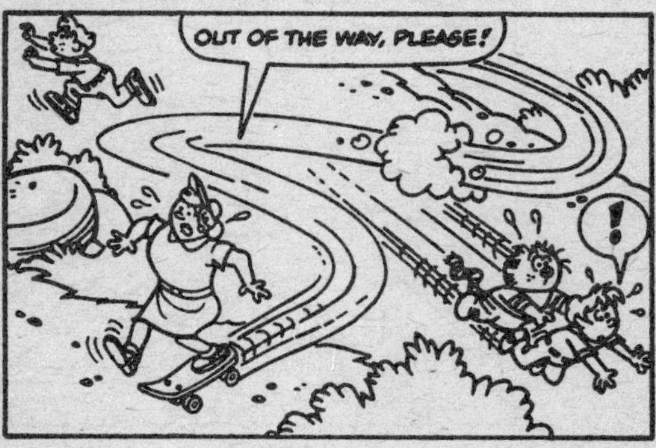
OUT OF THE WAY, PLEASE!
!

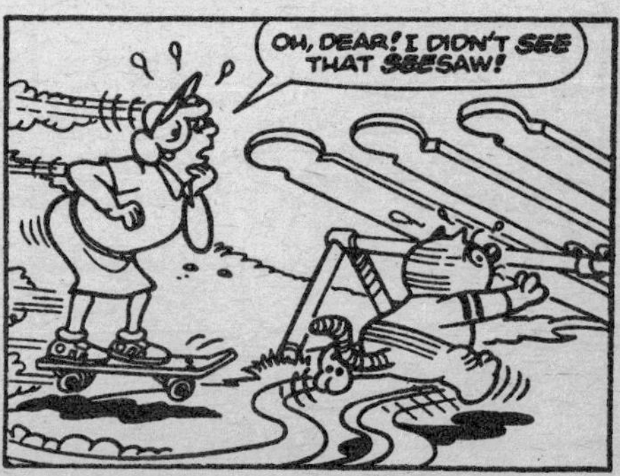
OH, DEAR! I DIDN'T SEE THAT SEESAW!

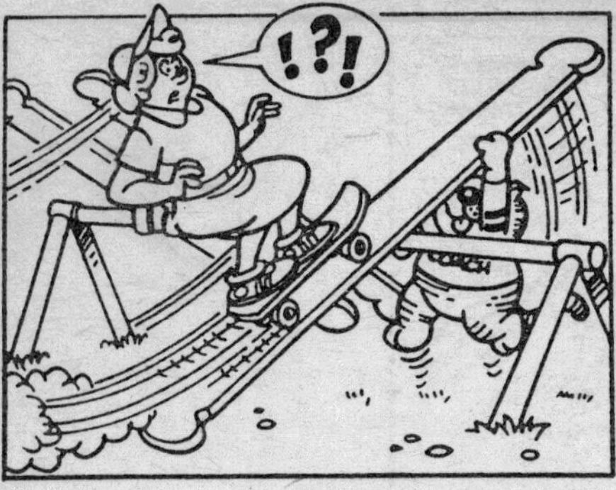
!?!

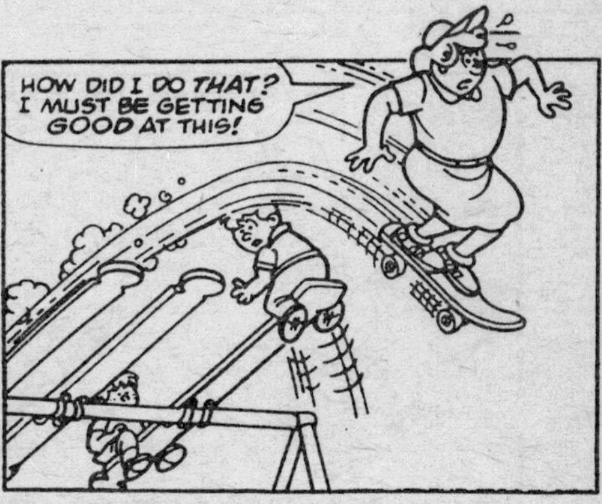
HOW DID I DO *THAT*? I MUST BE GETTING *GOOD* AT THIS!

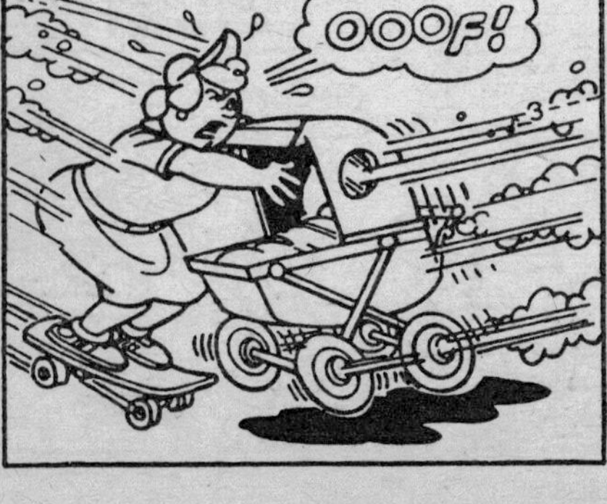
OOOF!

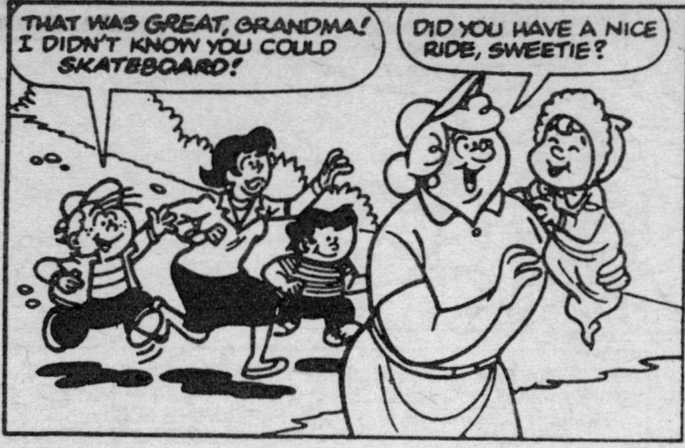
THAT WAS GREAT, GRANDMA! I DIDN'T KNOW YOU COULD SKATEBOARD!
DID YOU HAVE A NICE RIDE, SWEETIE?

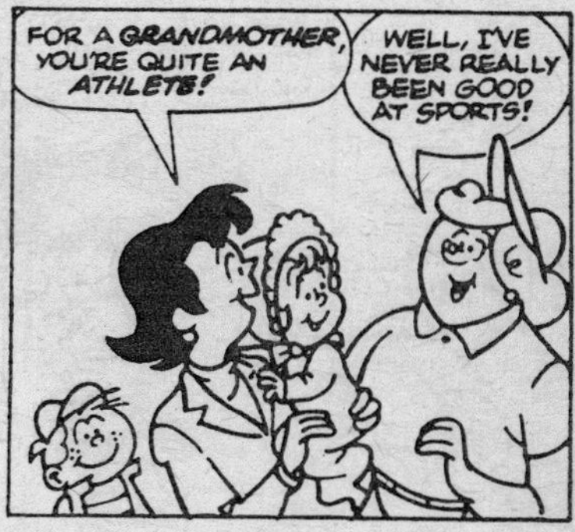
FOR A GRANDMOTHER, YOU'RE QUITE AN ATHLETE!
WELL, I'VE NEVER REALLY BEEN GOOD AT SPORTS!

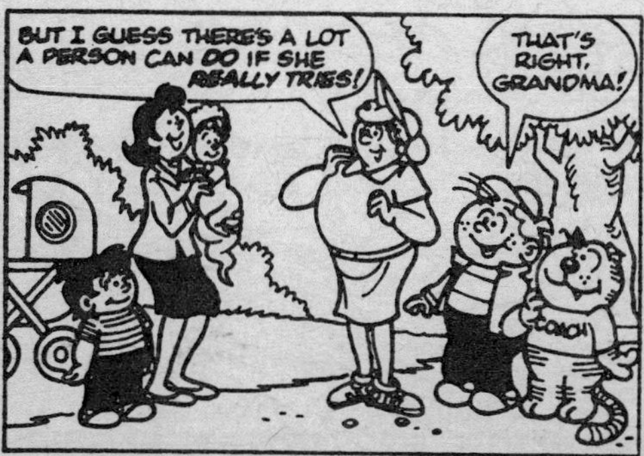
BUT I GUESS THERE'S A LOT A PERSON CAN DO IF SHE REALLY TRIES!
THAT'S RIGHT, GRANDMA!
COACH

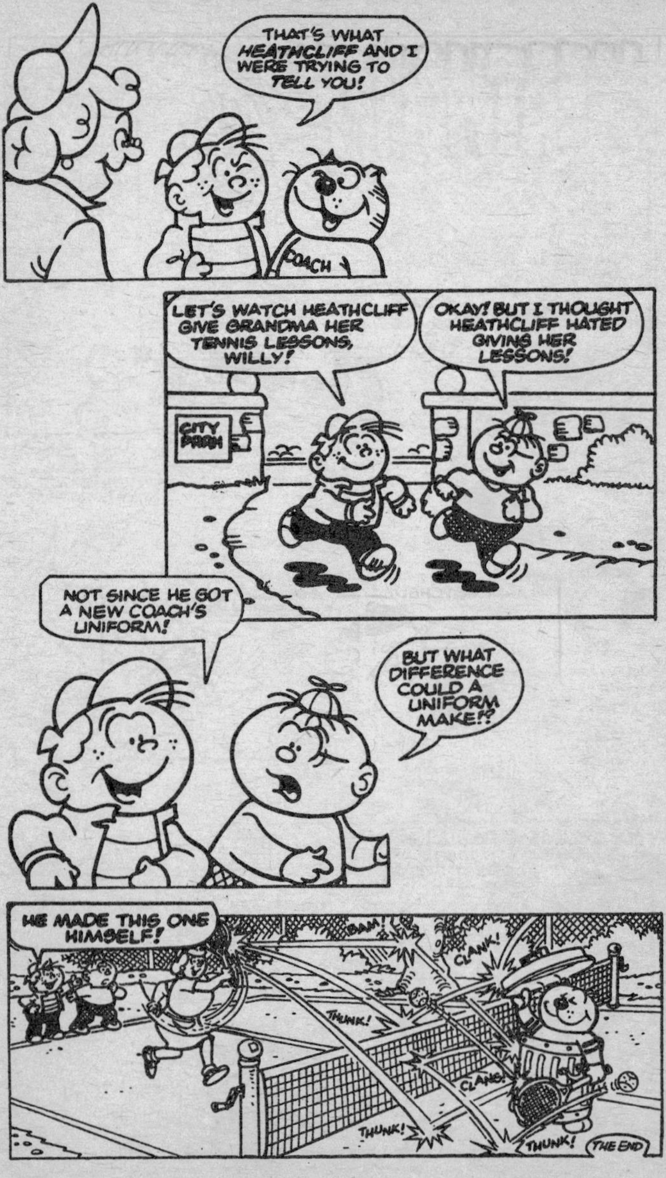
THAT'S WHAT HEATHCLIFF AND I WERE TRYING TO TELL YOU!
COACH
LET'S WATCH HEATHCLIFF GIVE GRANDMA HER TENNIS LESSONS, WILLY!
OKAY! BUT I THOUGHT HEATHCLIFF HATED GIVING HER LESSONS!
CITY PARK
NOT SINCE HE GOT A NEW COACH'S UNIFORM!
BUT WHAT DIFFERENCE COULD A UNIFORM MAKE!?
HE MADE THIS ONE HIMSELF!
BAM!
CLANK!
THUNK!
CLANG!
THUNK!
THUNK!
THE END

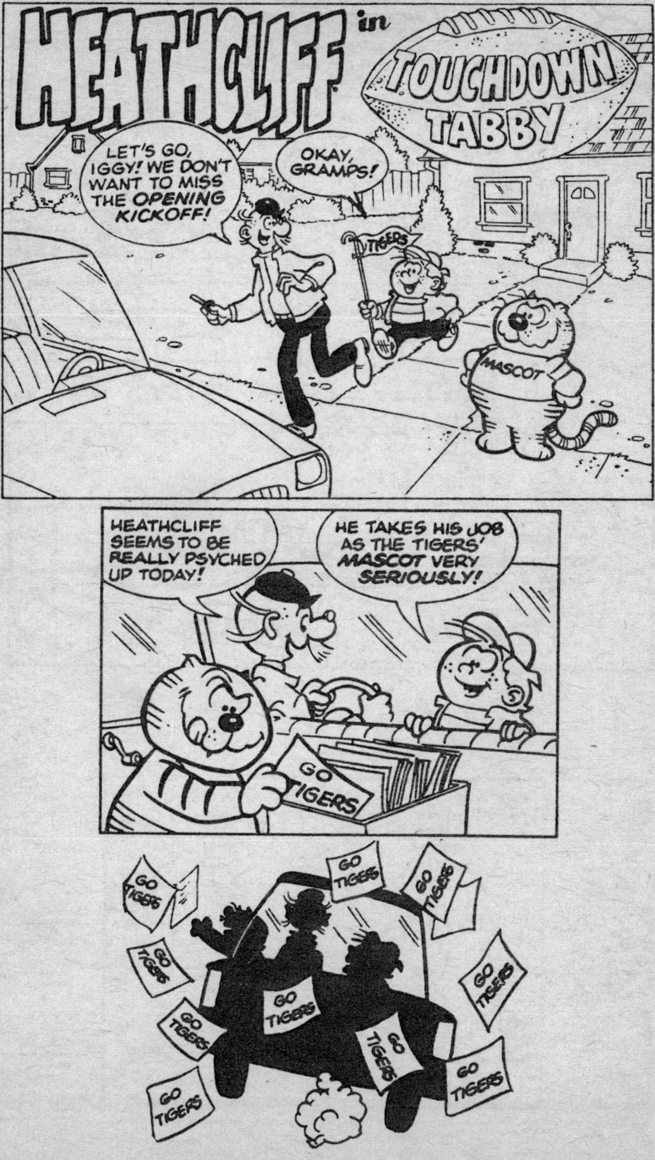
HEATHCLIFF in
TOUCHDOWN TABBY
LET'S GO, IGGY! WE DON'T WANT TO MISS THE OPENING KICKOFF!
OKAY, GRAMPS!
TIGERS
MASCOT
HEATHCLIFF SEEMS TO BE REALLY PSYCHED UP TODAY!
HE TAKES HIS JOB AS THE TIGERS' MASCOT VERY SERIOUSLY!
GO TIGERS
GO TIGERS
GO TIGERS
GO TIGERS
GO TIGERS
GO TIGERS
GO TIGERS
GO TIGERS
GO TIGERS
GO TIGERS
GO TIGERS

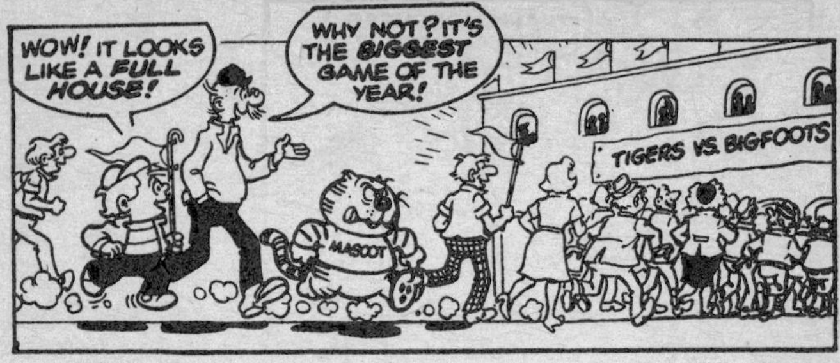
WOW! IT LOOKS LIKE A FULL HOUSE!
WHY NOT? IT'S THE BIGGEST GAME OF THE YEAR!
TIGERS VS. BIGFOOTS
MASCOT

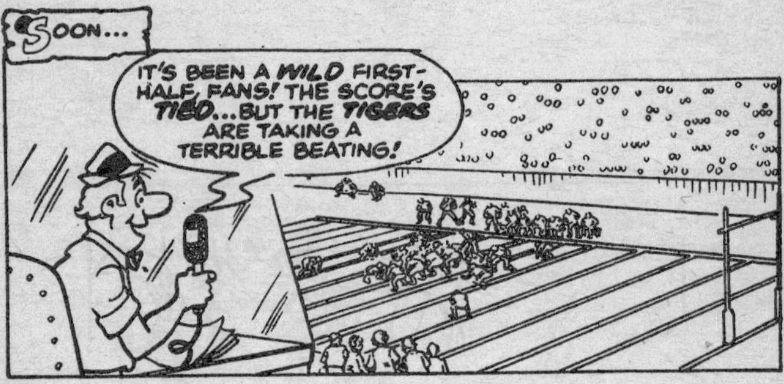
SOON...
IT'S BEEN A WILD FIRST-HALF, FANS! THE SCORE'S TIED...BUT THE TIGERS ARE TAKING A TERRIBLE BEATING!

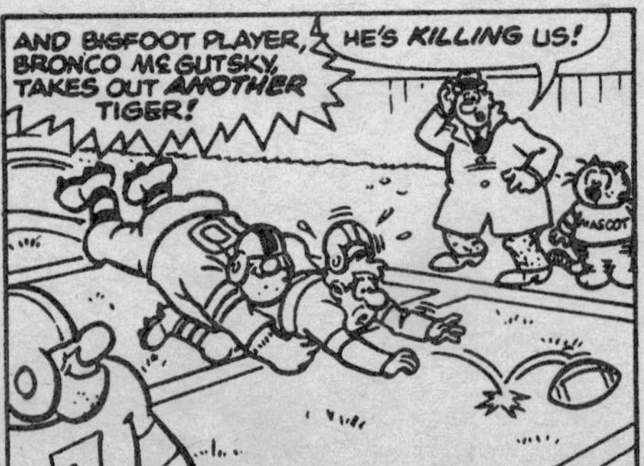
AND BIGFOOT PLAYER, BRONCO MCGUTSKY, TAKES OUT ANOTHER TIGER!
HE'S KILLING US!
MASCOT

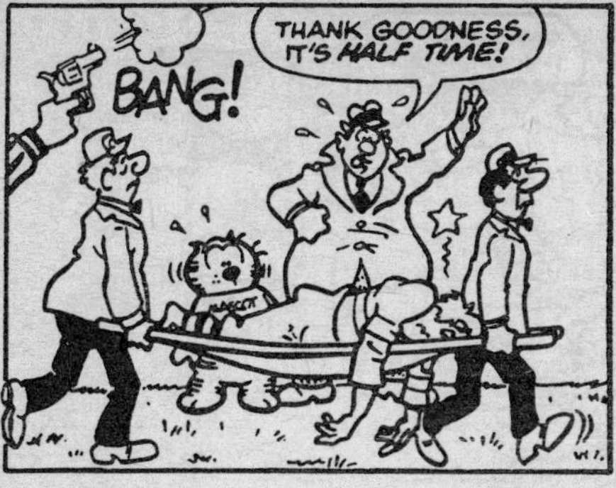
BANG!
THANK GOODNESS, IT'S HALF TIME!
MASCOT

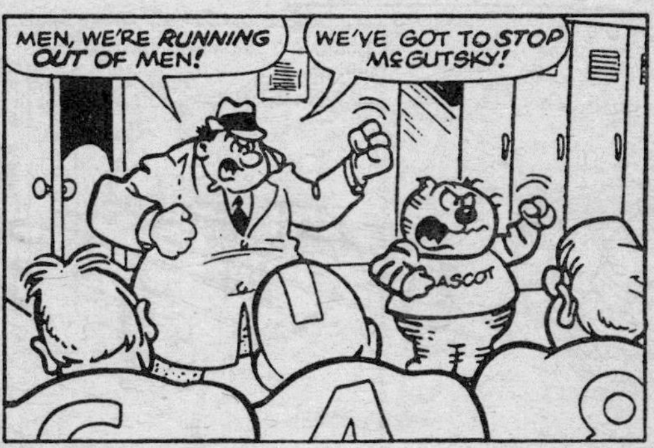
MEN, WE'RE RUNNING OUT OF MEN!
WE'VE GOT TO STOP McGUTSKY!
MASCOT

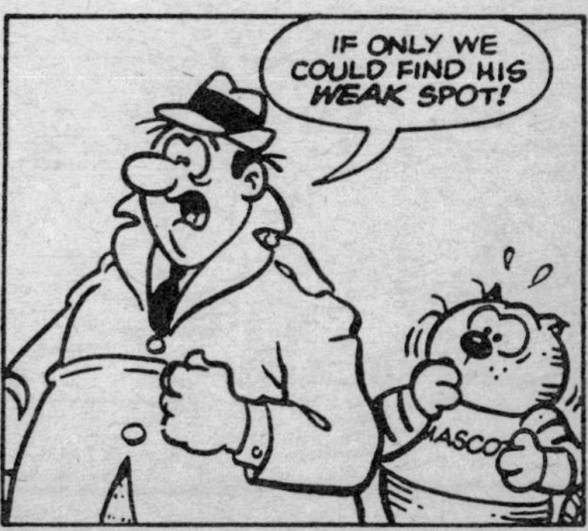
IF ONLY WE COULD FIND HIS WEAK SPOT!
MASCOT

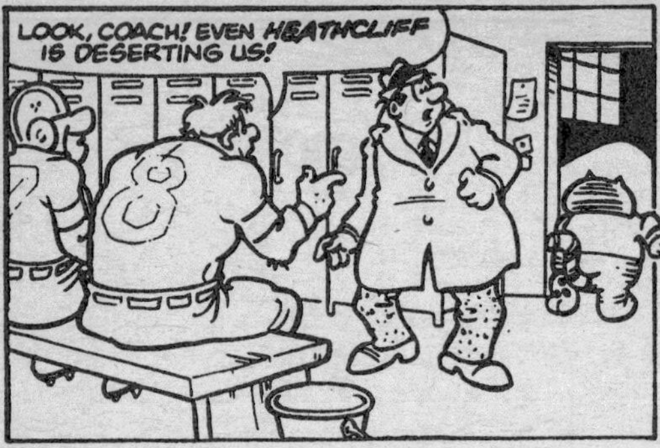
LOOK, COACH! EVEN HEATHCLIFF IS DESERTING US!

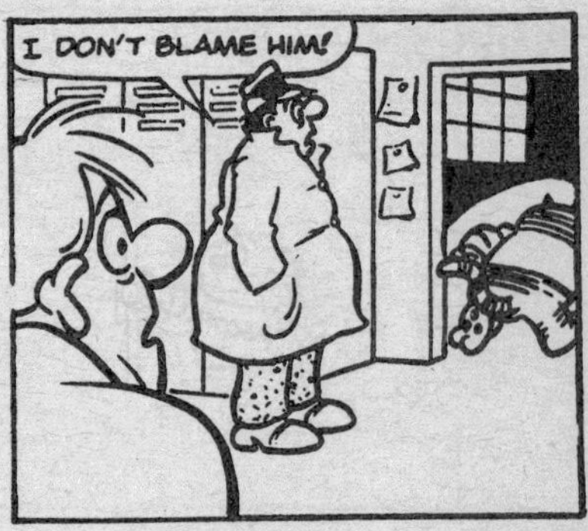
I DON'T BLAME HIM!

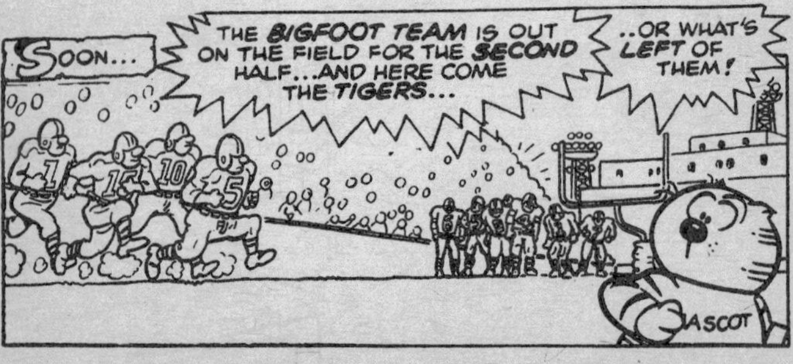
SOON...
THE BIGFOOT TEAM IS OUT ON THE FIELD FOR THE SECOND HALF...AND HERE COME THE TIGERS...
..OR WHAT'S LEFT OF THEM!
ASCOT

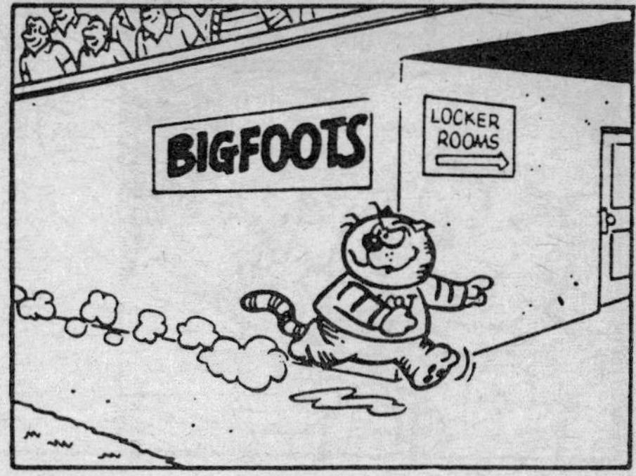
BIGFOOTS
LOCKER ROOMS

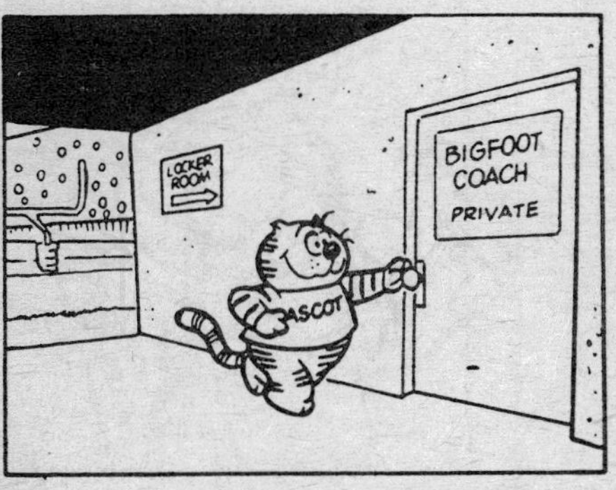
LOCKER ROOM
BIGFOOT COACH PRIVATE
MASCOT

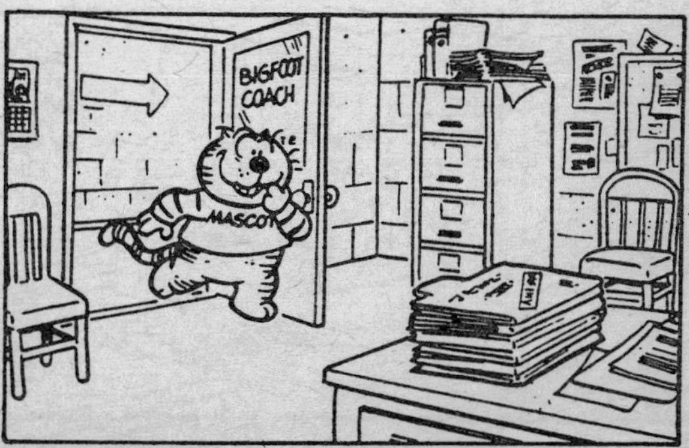
BIGFOOT COACH
MASCOT

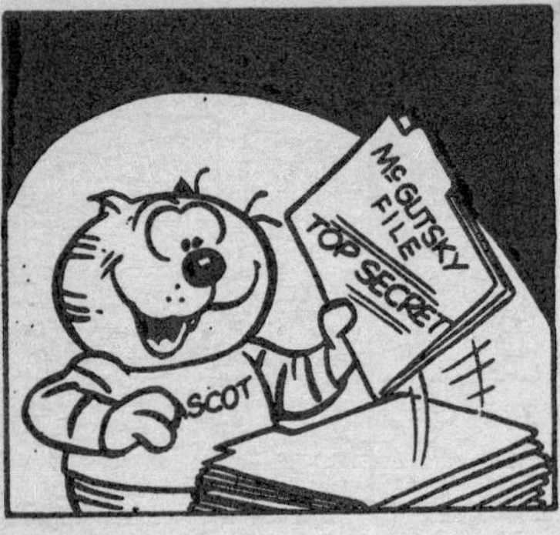
McGUTSKY FILE
TOP SECRET
ASCOT

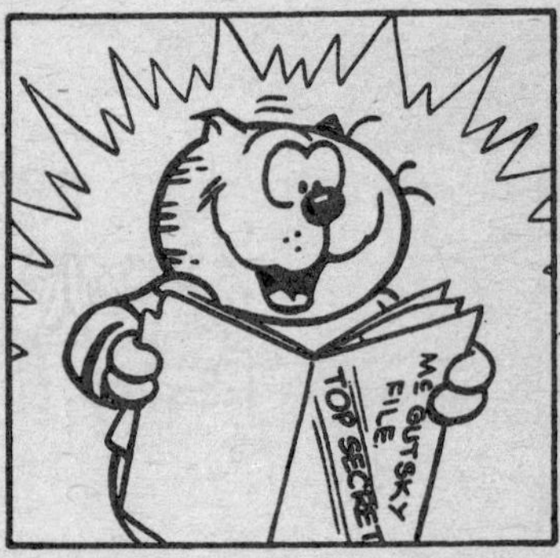
McGUTSKY FILE
TOP SECRET

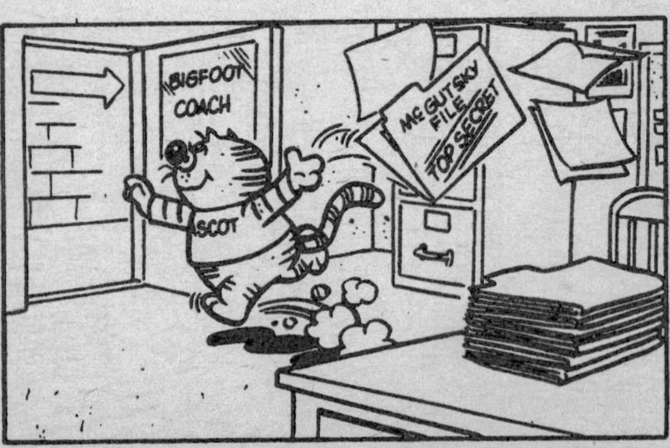
BIGFOOT COACH
McGUTSKY FILE
TOP SECRET
ASCOT

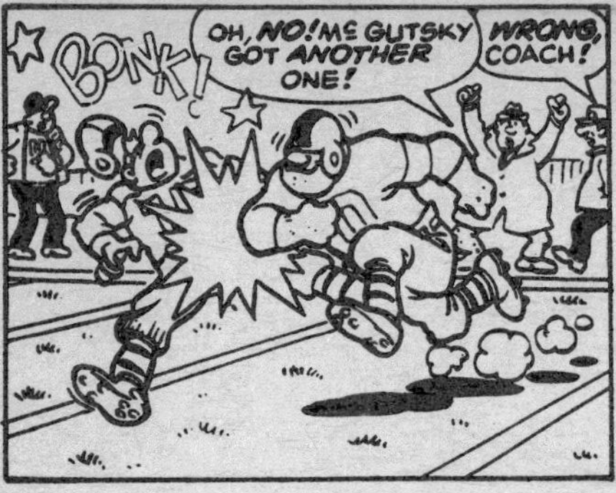
BONK!
OH, NO! McGUTSKY GOT ANOTHER ONE!
WRONG, COACH!

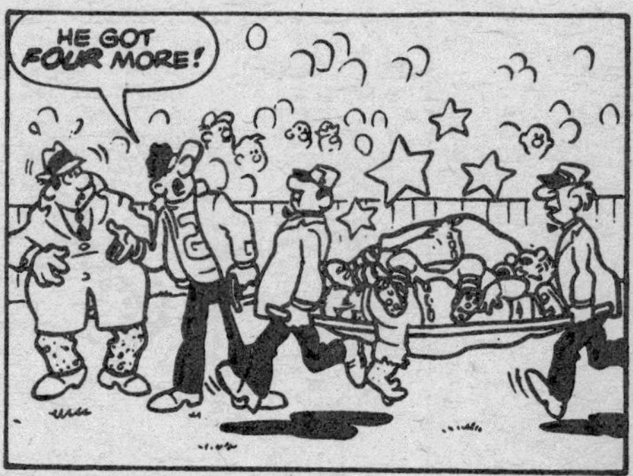
HE GOT FOUR MORE!

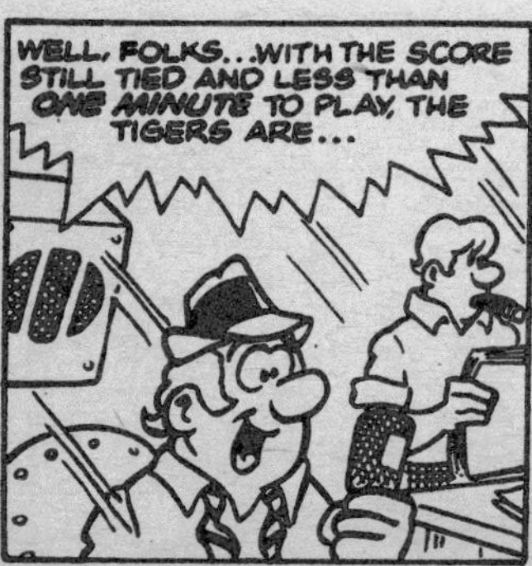
WELL, FOLKS...WITH THE SCORE STILL TIED AND LESS THAN ONE MINUTE TO PLAY, THE TIGERS ARE...

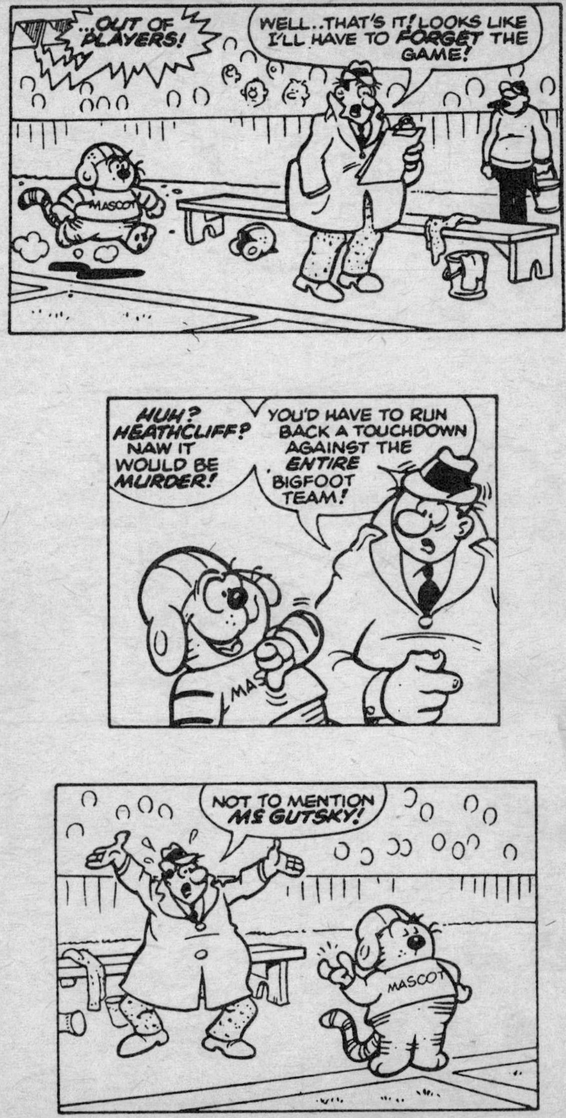
...OUT OF PLAYERS!
WELL..THAT'S IT! LOOKS LIKE I'LL HAVE TO FORGET THE GAME!
MASCOT
HUH? HEATHCLIFF? NAW IT WOULD BE MURDER!
YOU'D HAVE TO RUN BACK A TOUCHDOWN AGAINST THE ENTIRE BIGFOOT TEAM!
NOT TO MENTION McGUTSKY!
MASCOT

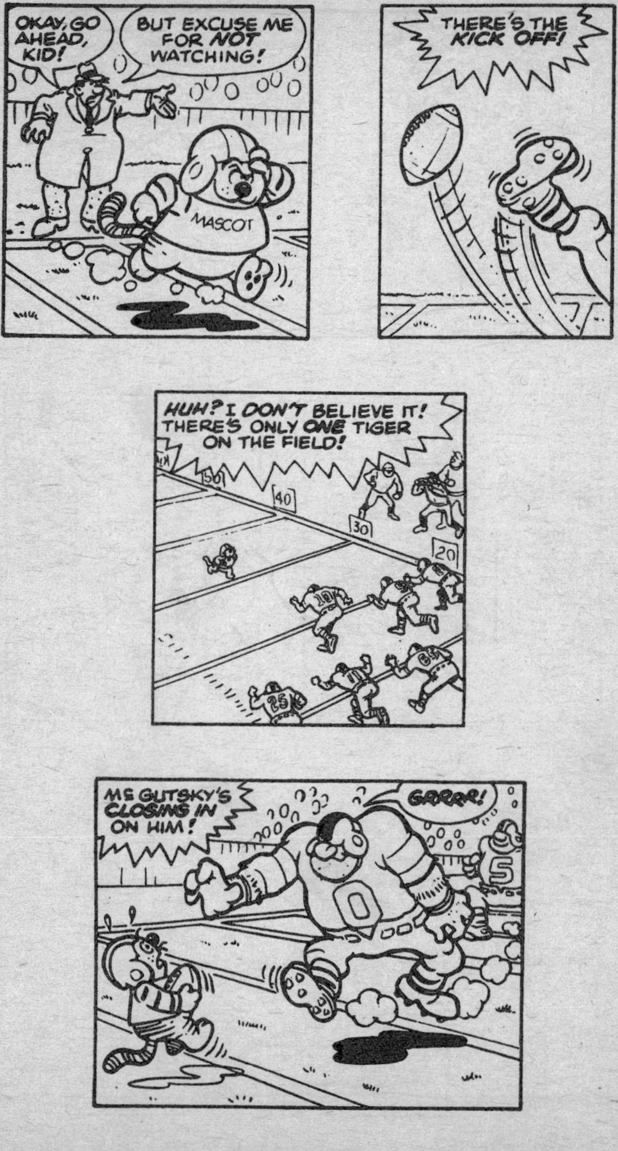
OKAY, GO AHEAD, KID!
BUT EXCUSE ME FOR NOT WATCHING!
MASCOT
THERE'S THE KICK OFF!
HUH? I DON'T BELIEVE IT! THERE'S ONLY ONE TIGER ON THE FIELD!
50
40
30
20
McGUTSKY'S CLOSING IN ON HIM!
GRRRR!

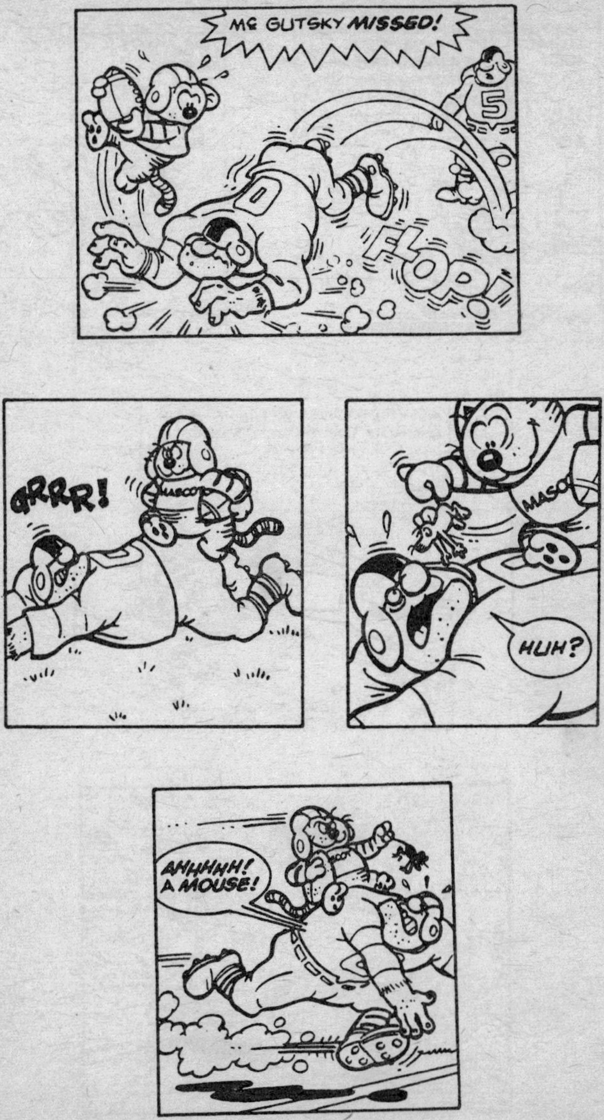
Mc GUTSKY MISSED!
FLOP!
GRRRR!
HUH?
AHHHHH! A MOUSE!

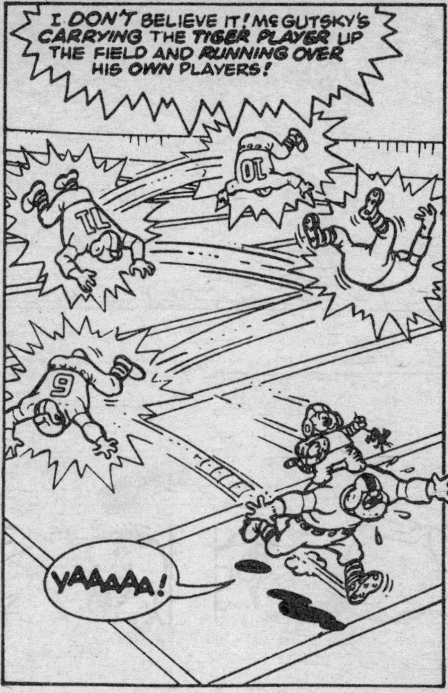
I DON'T BELIEVE IT! McGUTSKY'S CARRYING THE TIGER PLAYER UP THE FIELD AND RUNNING OVER HIS OWN PLAYERS!
YAAAAA!

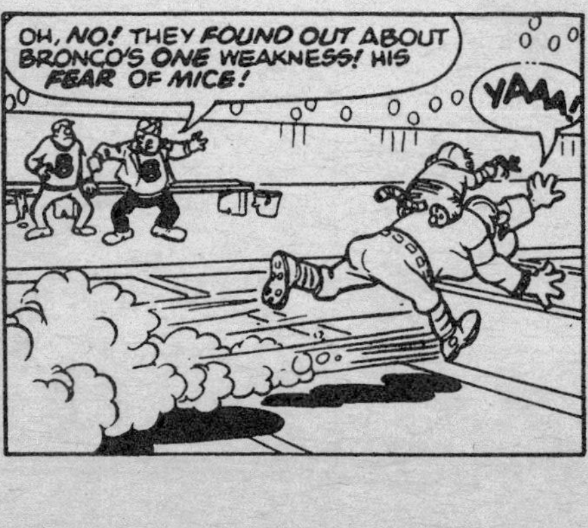
OH, NO! THEY FOUND OUT ABOUT BRONCO'S ONE WEAKNESS! HIS FEAR OF MICE!

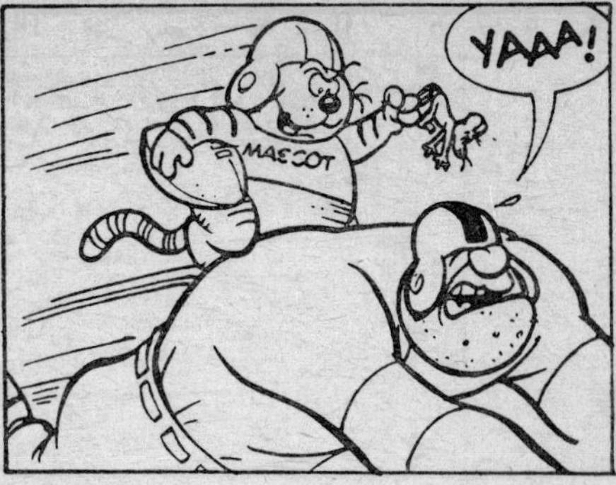
YAAA!
MASCOT

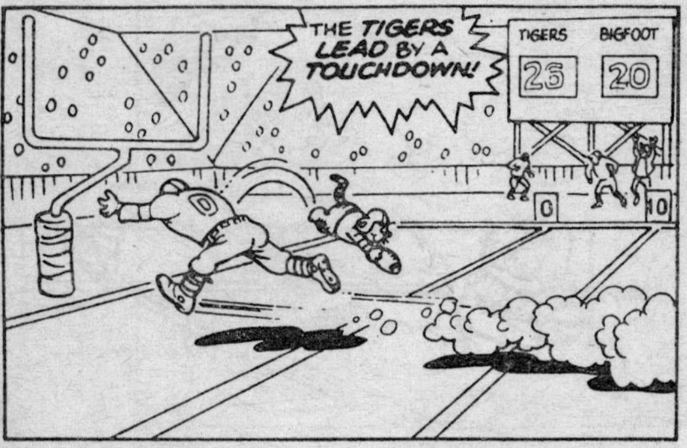
THE TIGERS LEAD BY A TOUCHDOWN!
TIGERS
BIGFOOT
26
20

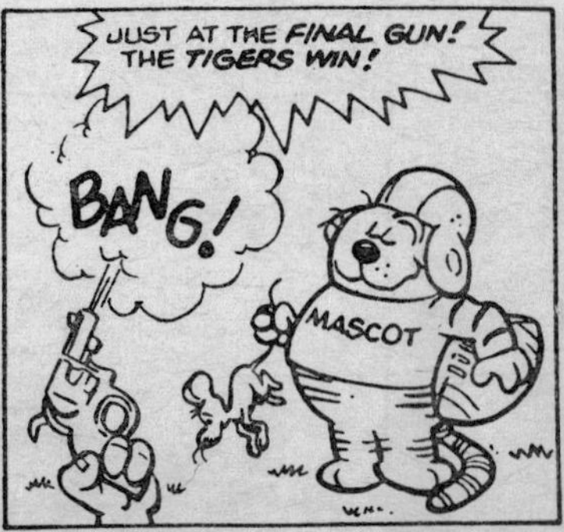
JUST AT THE FINAL GUN! THE TIGERS WIN!
BANG!
MASCOT

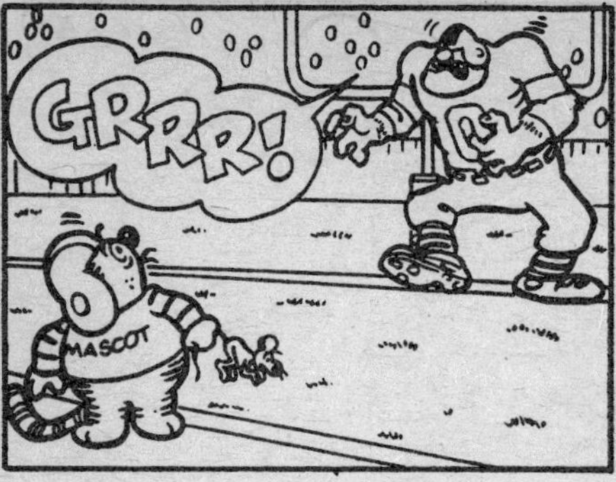
GRRR!
MASCOT

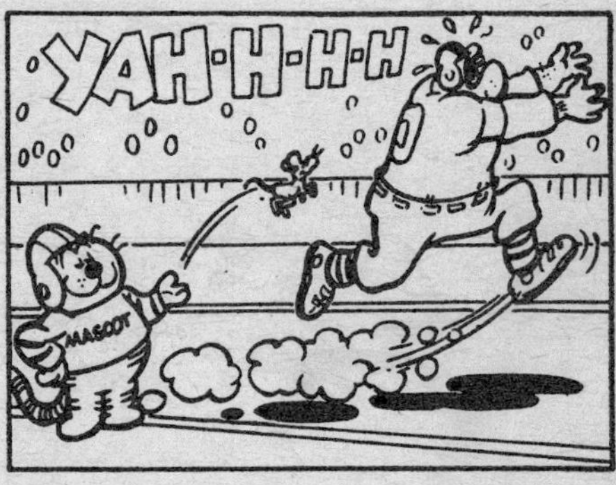
YAH-H-H-H
MASCOT

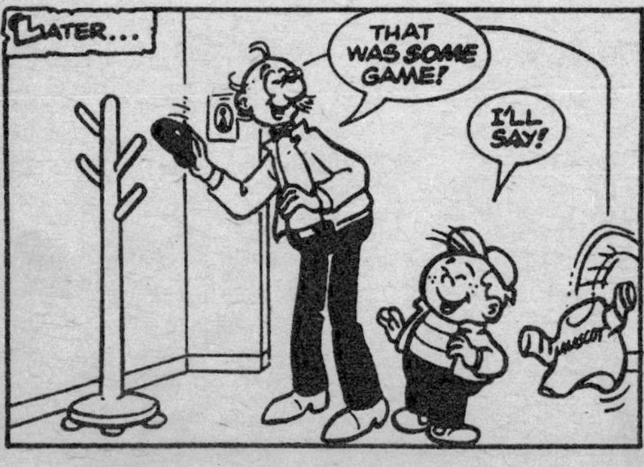
LATER...
THAT WAS SOME GAME!
I'LL SAY!
MASCOT

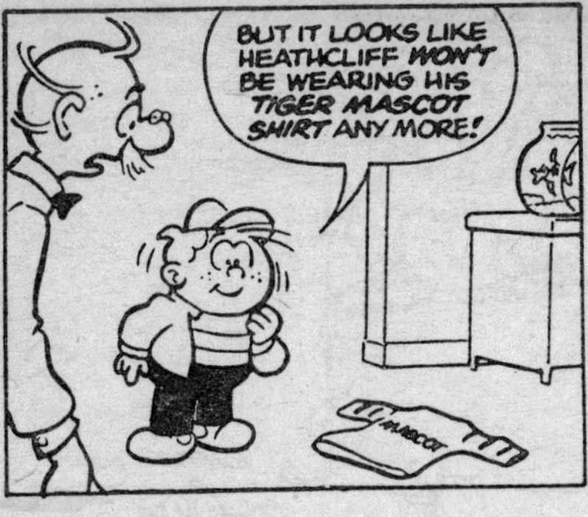
BUT IT LOOKS LIKE HEATHCLIFF *WON'T* BE WEARING HIS *TIGER MASCOT SHIRT* ANY MORE!

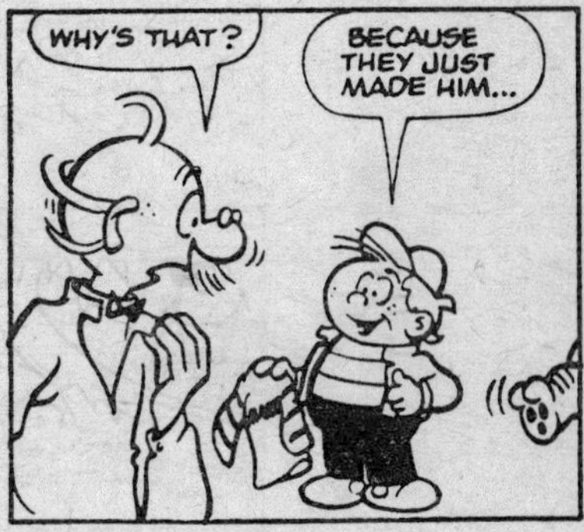
WHY'S THAT?
BECAUSE THEY JUST MADE HIM...

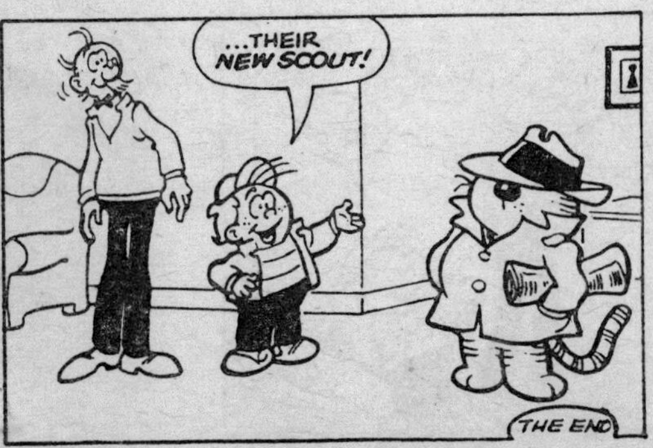
...THEIR *NEW SCOUT!*
THE END

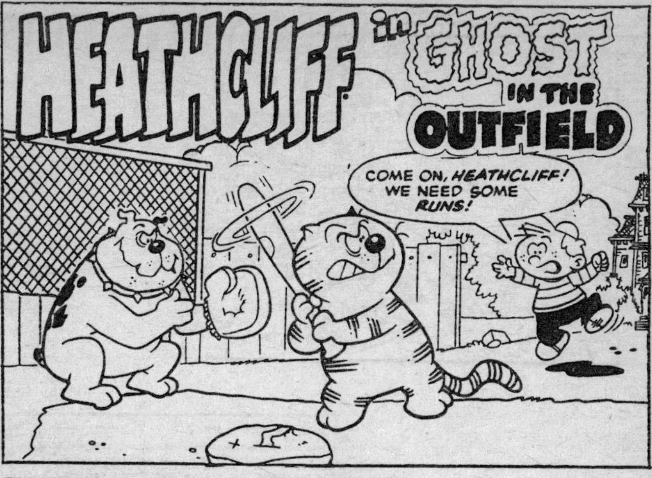
HEATHCLIFF in GHOST IN THE OUTFIELD
COME ON, HEATHCLIFF! WE NEED SOME RUNS!

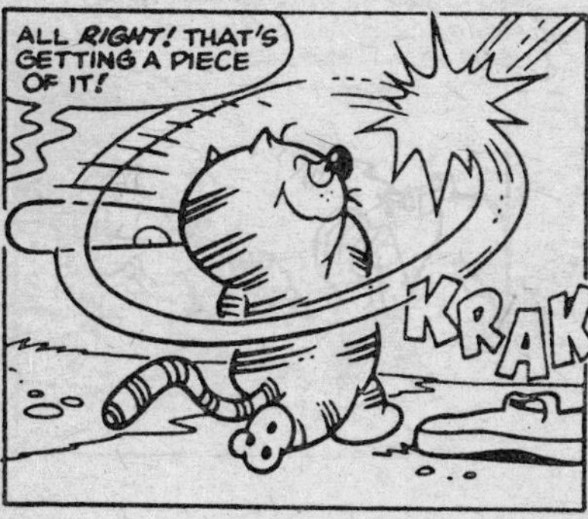
ALL RIGHT! THAT'S GETTING A PIECE OF IT!
KRAK-

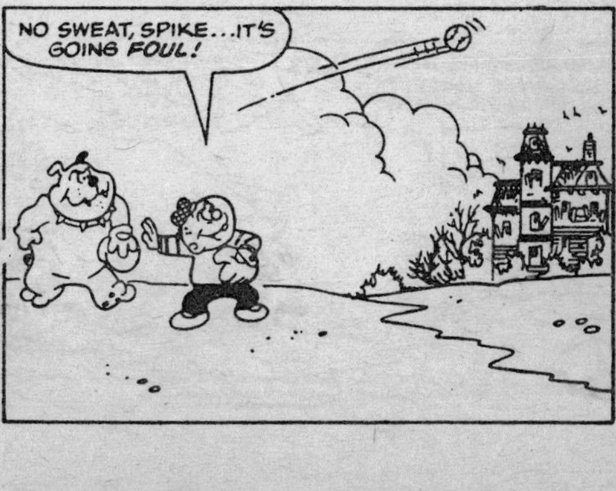
NO SWEAT, SPIKE...IT'S GOING FOUL!

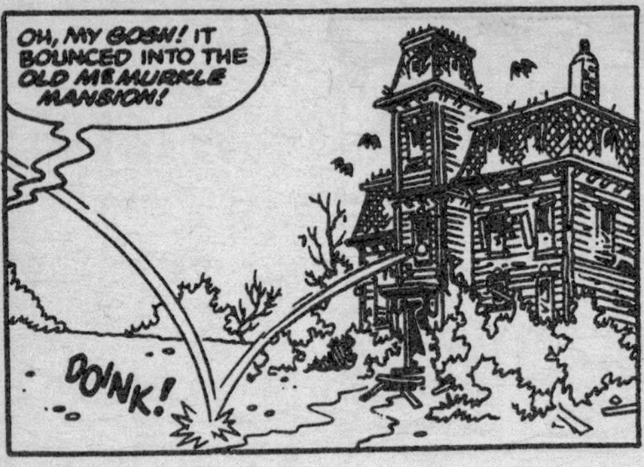
OH, MY GOSH! IT BOUNCED INTO THE OLD McMURKLE MANSION!
DOINK!

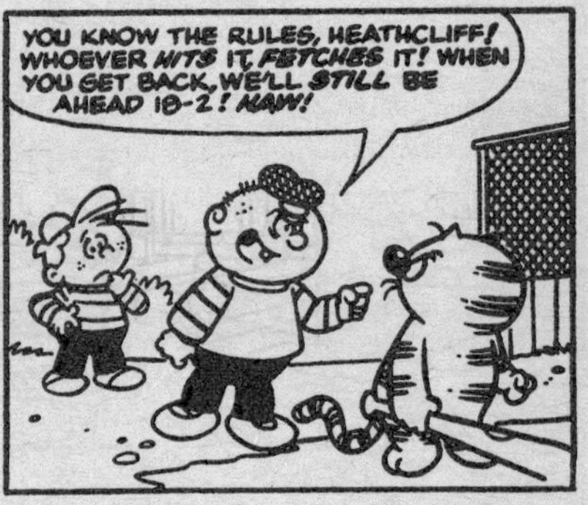
YOU KNOW THE RULES, HEATHCLIFF! WHOEVER HITS IT FETCHES IT! WHEN YOU GET BACK, WE'LL STILL BE AHEAD 18-2! HAW!

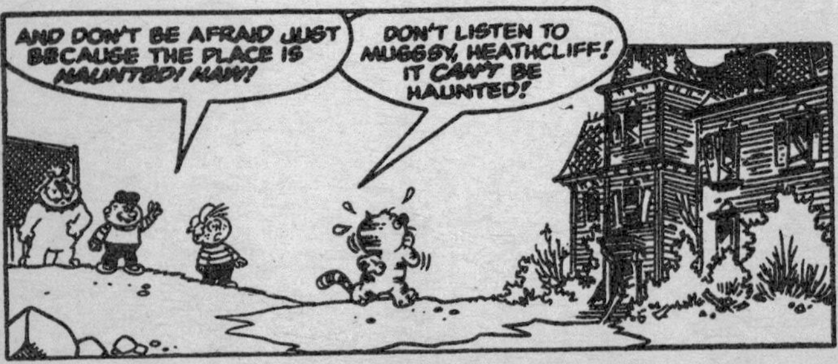
AND DON'T BE AFRAID JUST BECAUSE THE PLACE IS HAUNTED! HAW!
DON'T LISTEN TO MUGGSY, HEATHCLIFF! IT CAN'T BE HAUNTED!

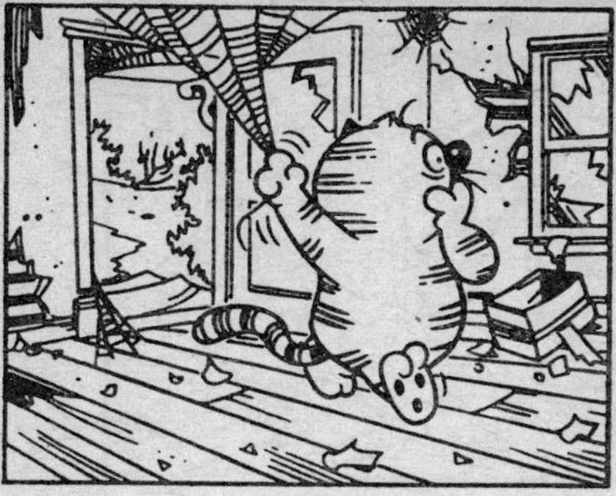

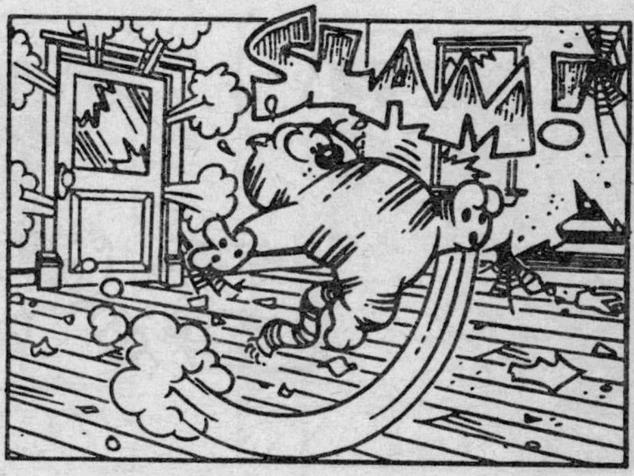
SLAM!

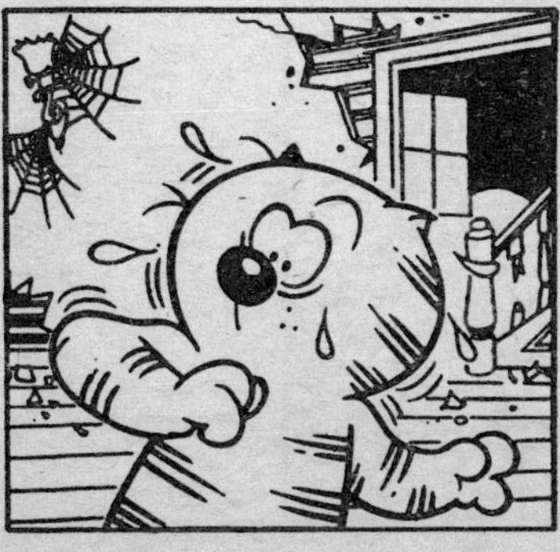

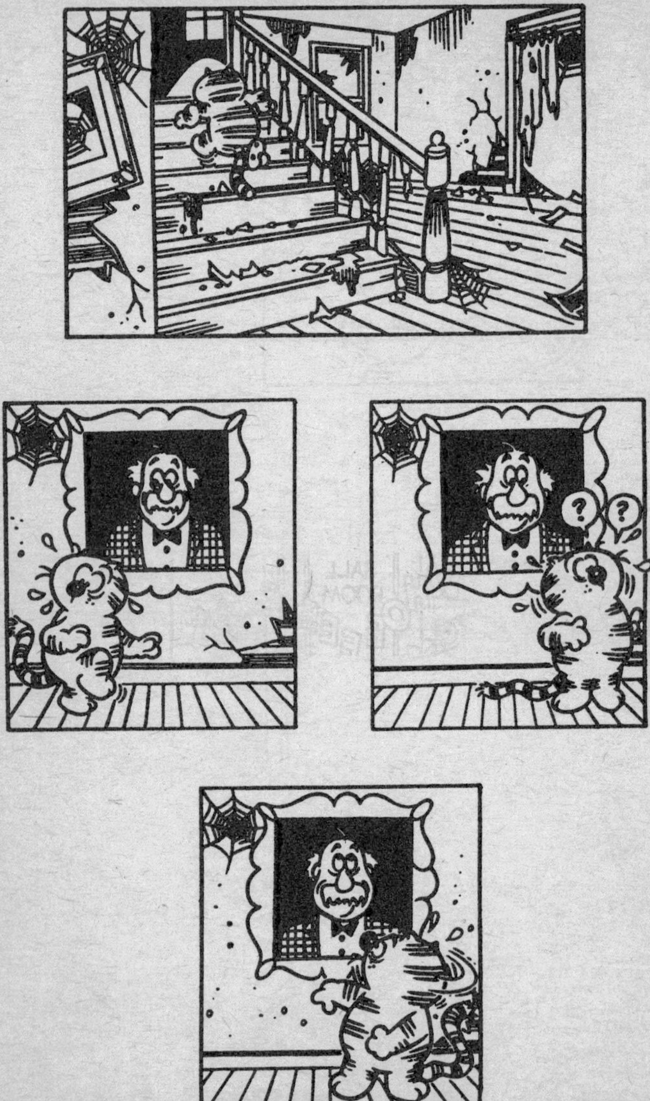
?
?

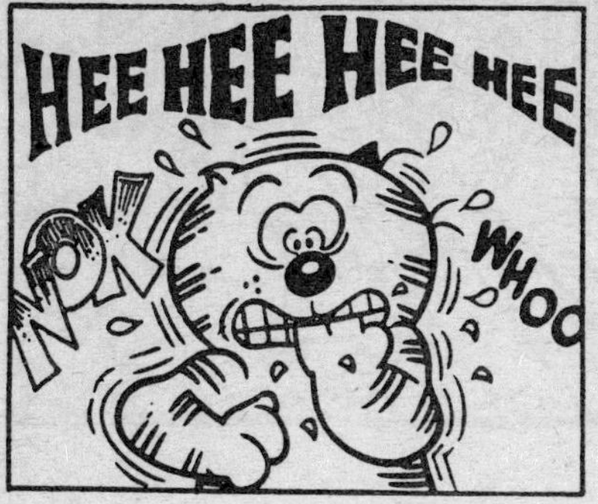
HEE HEE HEE HEE
NOK
WHOO

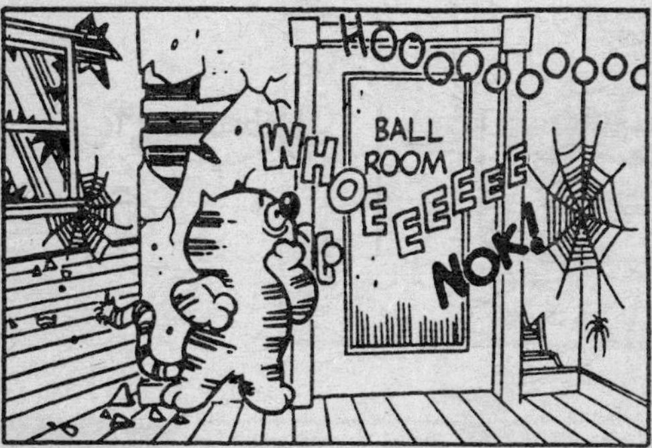
HOOOOOOOOOOO
BALL ROOM
WHOEEEEEEE
NOK!

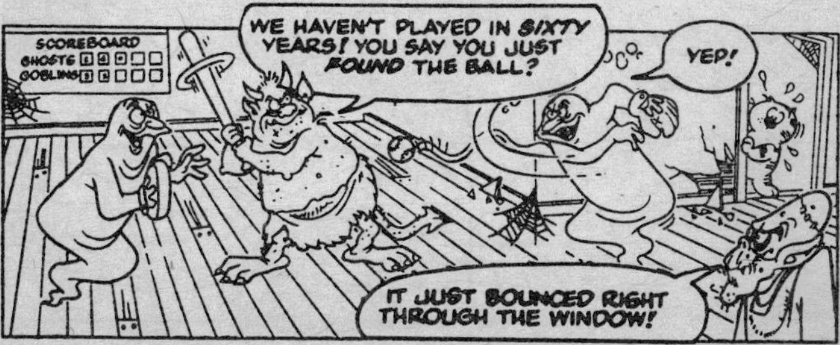
SCOREBOARD
GHOSTS
GOBLINS
WE HAVEN'T PLAYED IN *SIXTY* YEARS! YOU SAY YOU JUST *FOUND* THE BALL?
YEP!
IT JUST BOUNCED RIGHT THROUGH THE WINDOW!

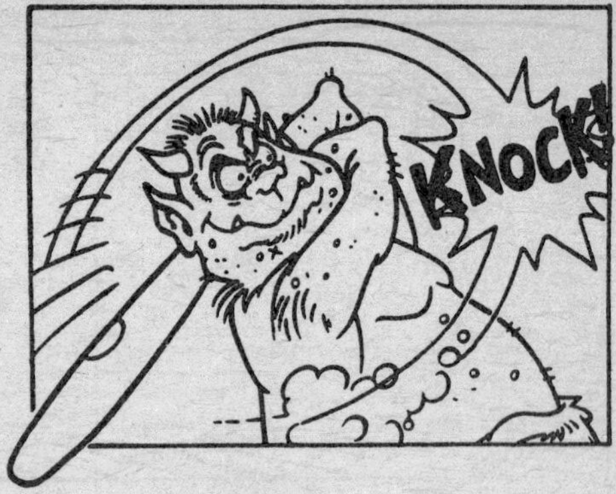
KNOCK!

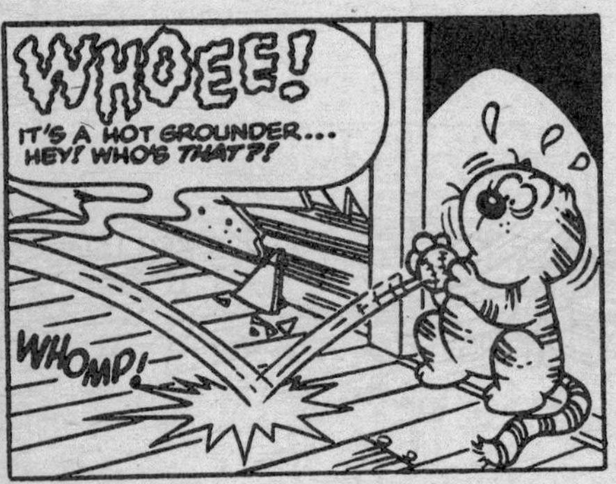
WHOEE!
IT'S A HOT GROUNDER...
HEY! WHO'S THAT?!
WHOMP!

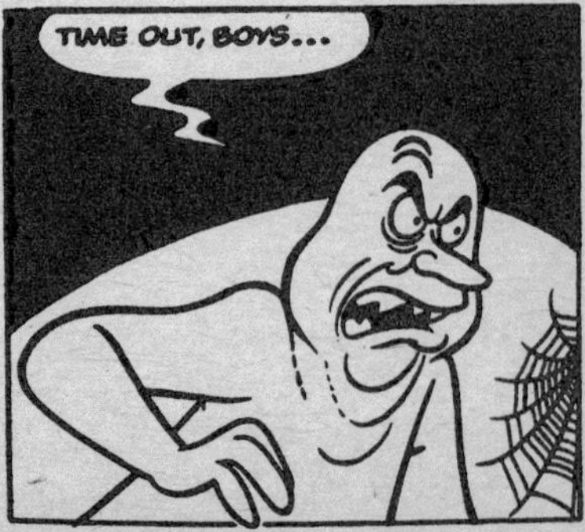
TIME OUT, BOYS...

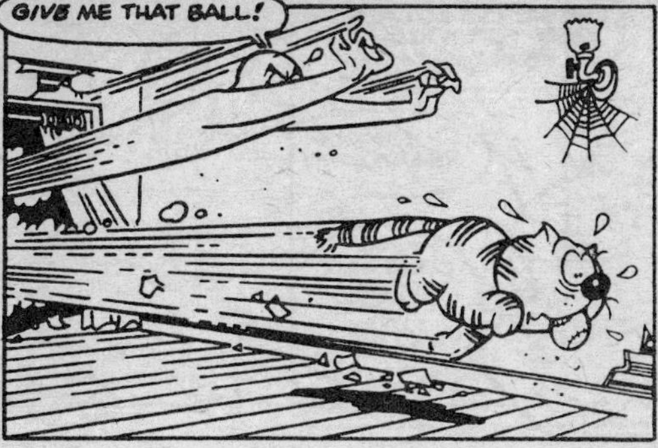
GIVE ME THAT BALL!

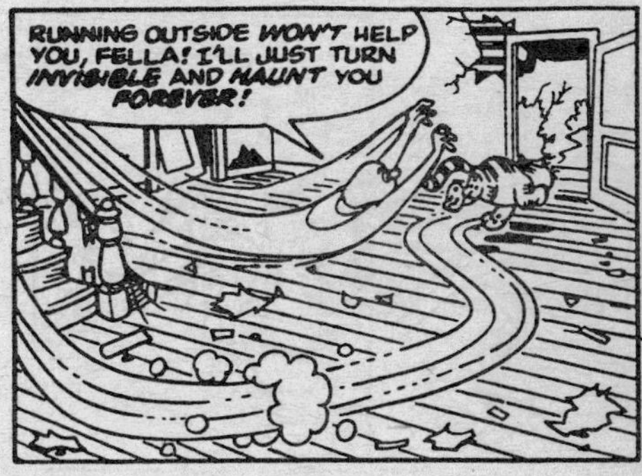
RUNNING OUTSIDE WON'T HELP YOU, FELLA! I'LL JUST TURN INVISIBLE AND HAUNT YOU FOREVER!

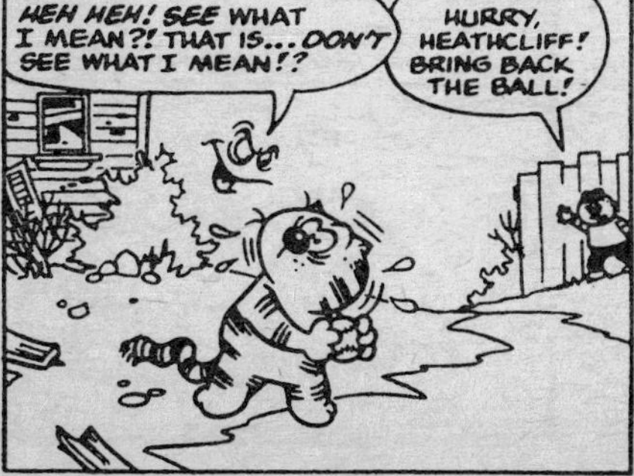
HEH HEH! SEE WHAT I MEAN?! THAT IS... DON'T SEE WHAT I MEAN!?
HURRY, HEATHCLIFF! BRING BACK THE BALL!

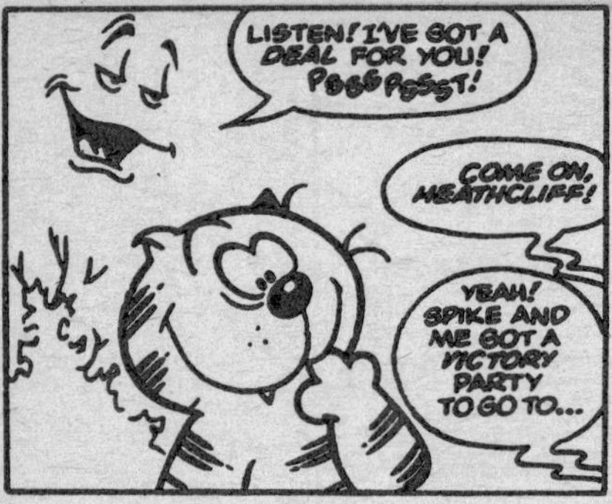
LISTEN! I'VE GOT A DEAL FOR YOU! PSSSPSSST!
COME ON, HEATHCLIFF!
YEAH! SPIKE AND ME GOT A VICTORY PARTY TO GO TO...

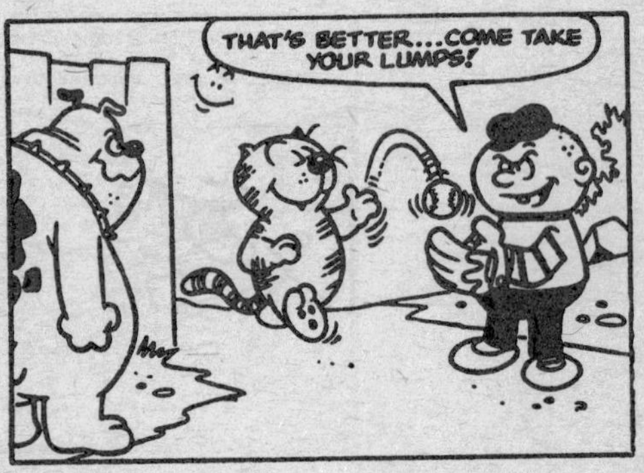
THAT'S BETTER....COME TAKE YOUR LUMPS!

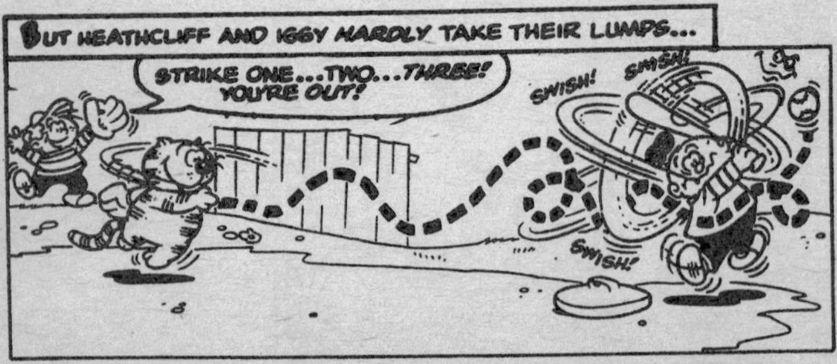
BUT HEATHCLIFF AND IGGY HARDLY TAKE THEIR LUMPS...
STRIKE ONE...TWO...THREE! YOU'RE OUT!
SWISH!
SWISH!
SWISH!

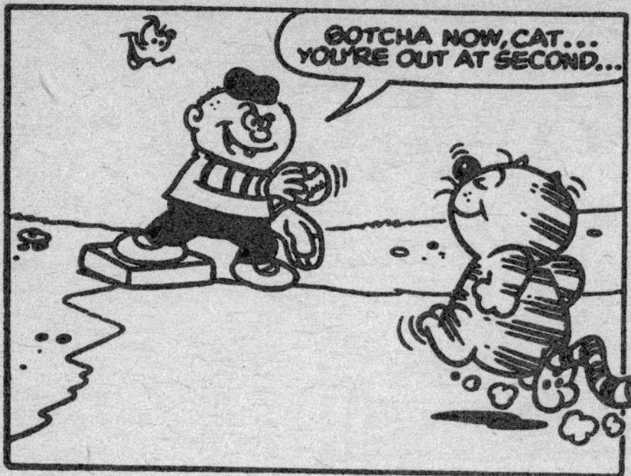
GOTCHA NOW, CAT...
YOU'RE OUT AT SECOND...

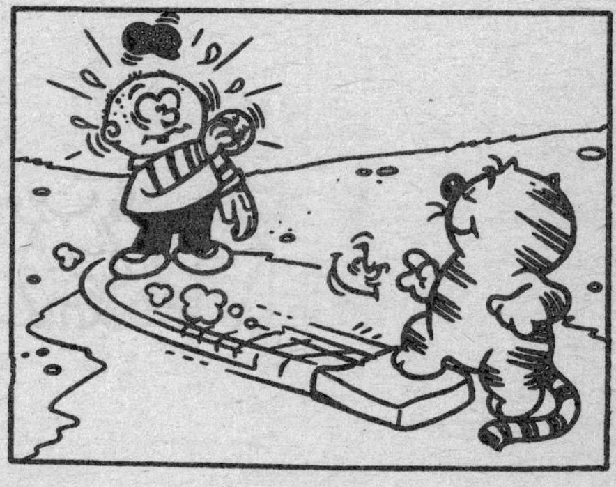

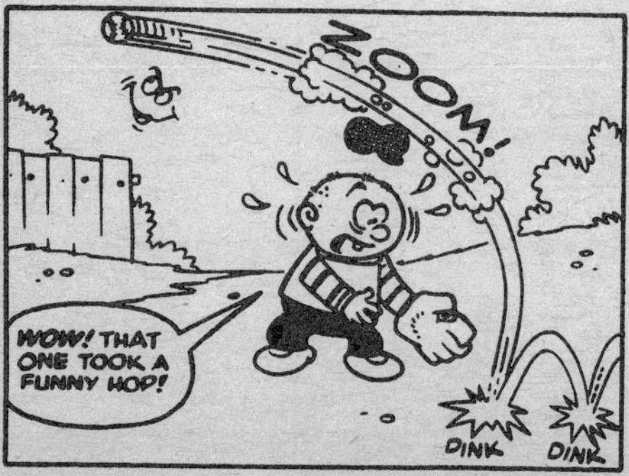
ZOOM!
WOW! THAT ONE TOOK A FUNNY HOP!
DINK
DINK

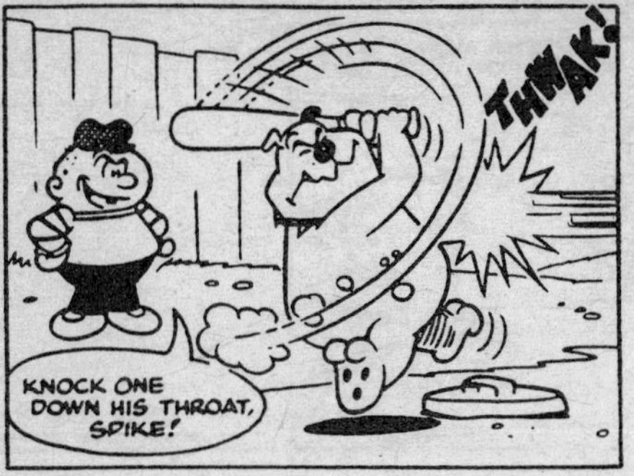
THWAK!
KNOCK ONE DOWN HIS THROAT, SPIKE!

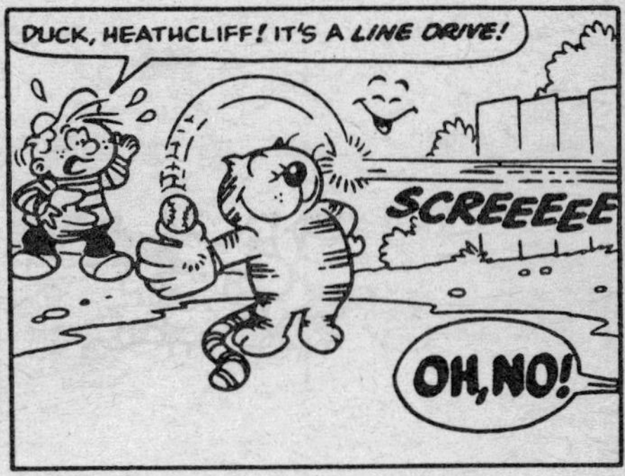
DUCK, HEATHCLIFF! IT'S A *LINE DRIVE!*
SCREEEEEE
OH, NO!

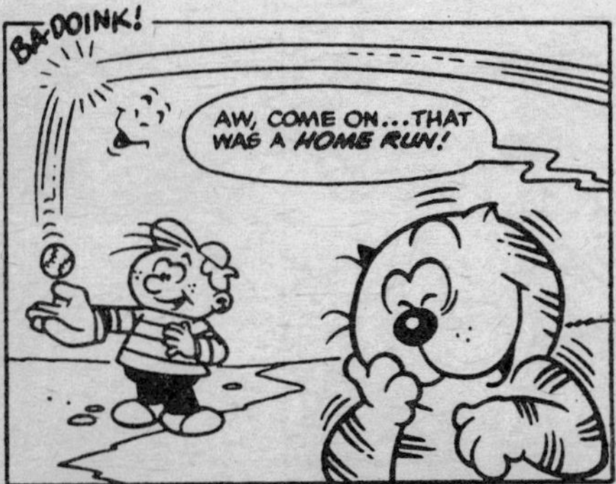
BA-DOINK!
AW, COME ON... THAT WAS A *HOME RUN!*

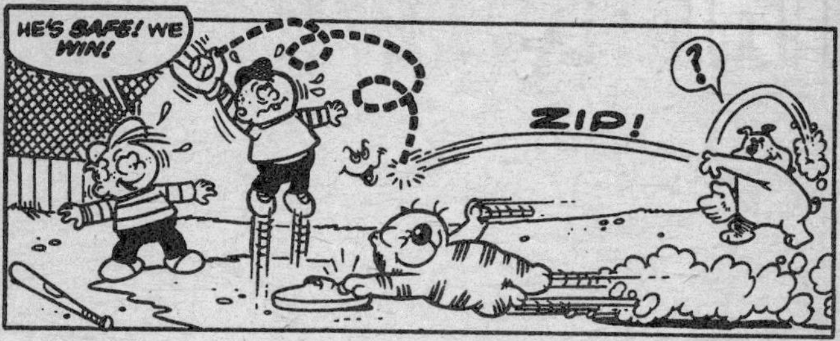
HE'S SAFE! WE WIN!
?
ZIP!

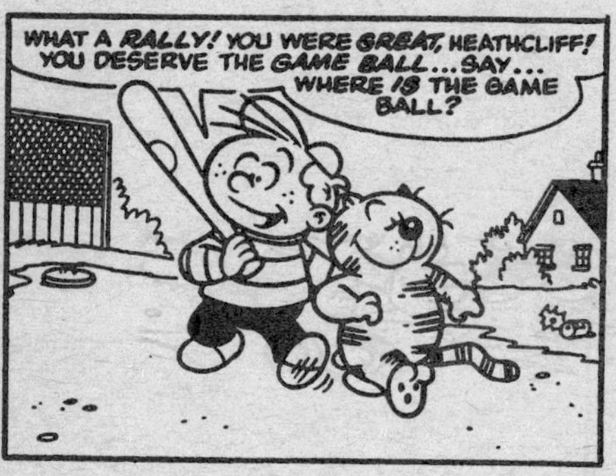
WHAT A RALLY! YOU WERE GREAT, HEATHCLIFF! YOU DESERVE THE GAME BALL...SAY... WHERE IS THE GAME BALL?

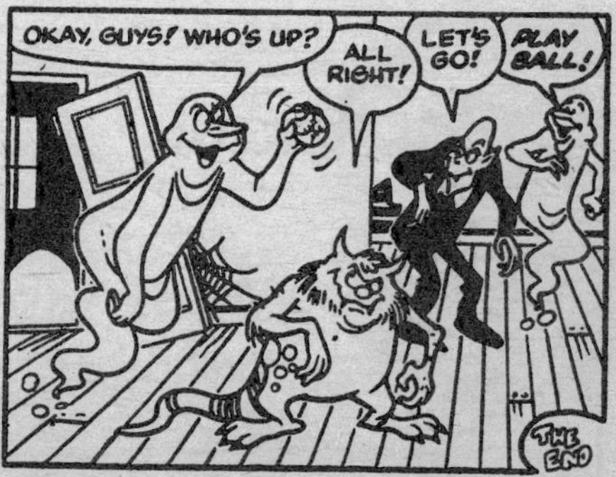
OKAY, GUYS! WHO'S UP?
ALL RIGHT!
LET'S GO!
PLAY BALL!
THE END

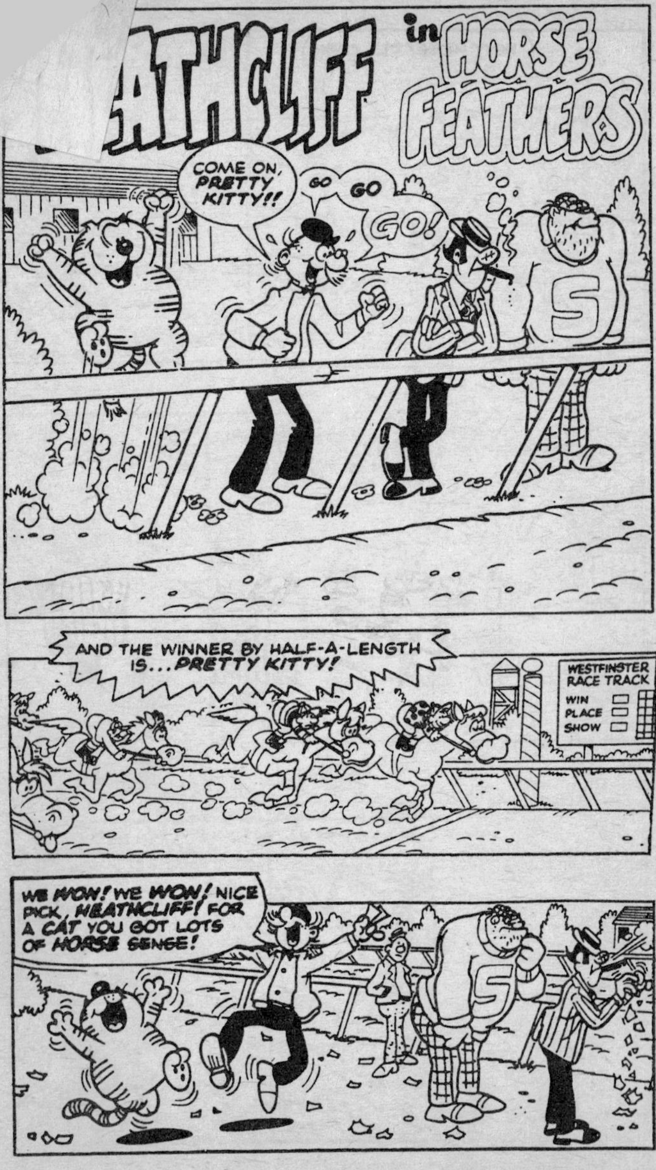
EATHCLIFF in HORSE FEATHERS
COME ON, PRETTY KITTY!!
GO GO GO!
S
AND THE WINNER BY HALF-A-LENGTH IS...PRETTY KITTY!
WESTFINSTER RACE TRACK
WIN
PLACE
SHOW
WE WON! WE WON! NICE PICK, HEATHCLIFF! FOR A CAT YOU GOT LOTS OF HORSE SENSE!
S

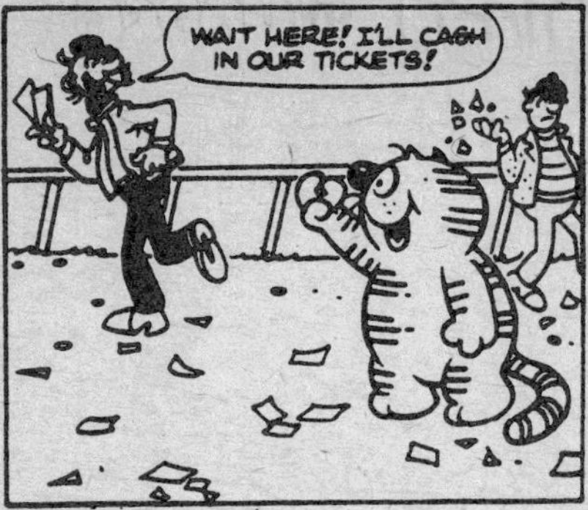
WAIT HERE! I'LL CASH IN OUR TICKETS!

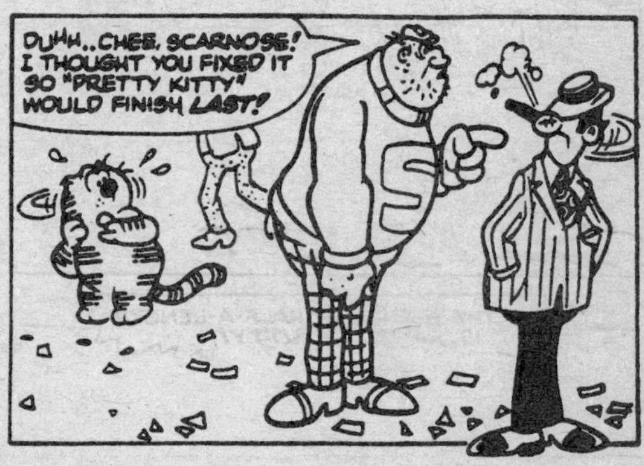
DUHH..CHEE, SCARNOSE! I THOUGHT YOU FIXED IT SO "PRETTY KITTY" WOULD FINISH LAST!

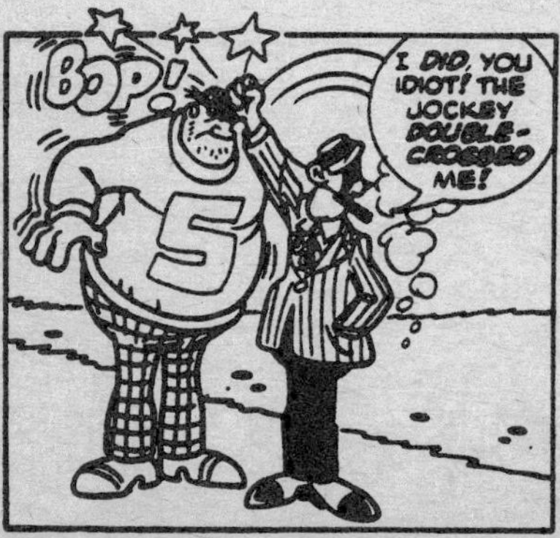
BOP!
I DID, YOU IDIOT! THE JOCKEY DOUBLE-CROSSED ME!

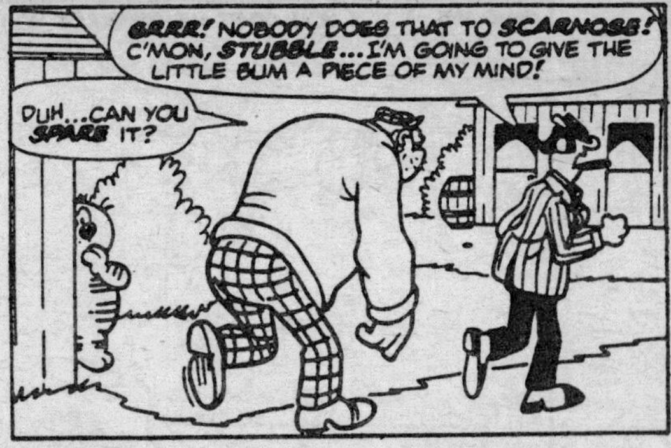
GRRR! NOBODY DOES THAT TO SCARNOSE! C'MON, STUBBLE... I'M GOING TO GIVE THE LITTLE BUM A PIECE OF MY MIND!
DUH...CAN YOU SPARE IT?

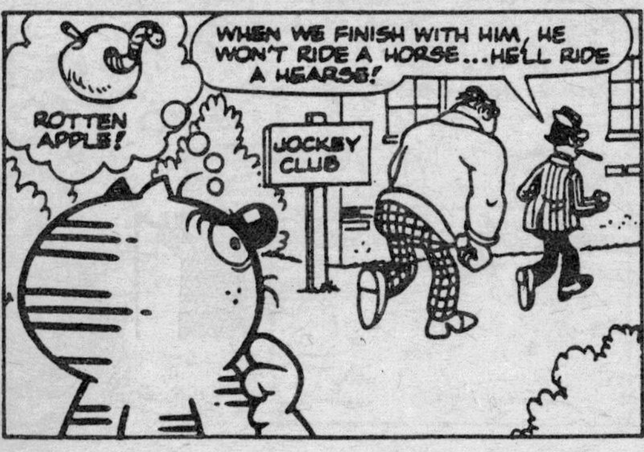
ROTTEN APPLE!
WHEN WE FINISH WITH HIM, HE WON'T RIDE A HORSE...HE'LL RIDE A HEARSE!
JOCKEY CLUB

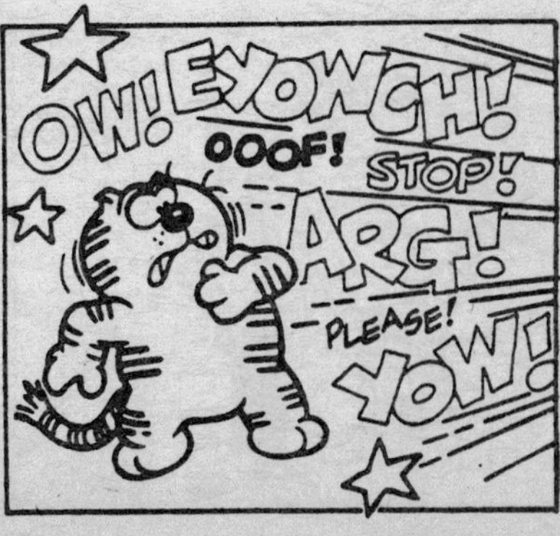
OW! EYOWCH!
OOOF!
STOP!
ARG!
PLEASE!
YOW!

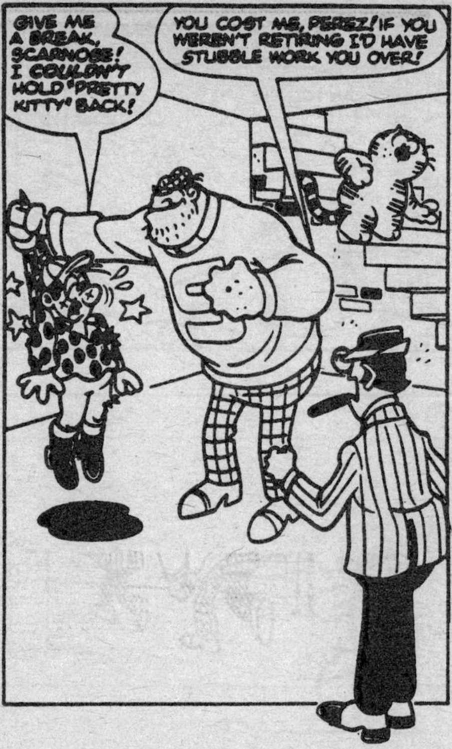
GIVE ME A BREAK, SCARNOSE! I COULDN'T HOLD "PRETTY KITTY" BACK!
YOU COST ME, PEREZ! IF YOU WEREN'T RETIRING I'D HAVE STUBBLE WORK YOU OVER!

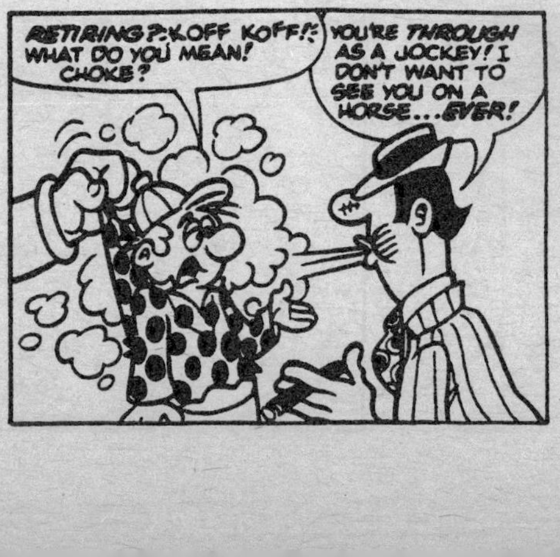
RETIRING?! KOFF KOFF!! WHAT DO YOU MEAN! CHOKE?
YOU'RE THROUGH AS A JOCKEY! I DON'T WANT TO SEE YOU ON A HORSE...EVER!

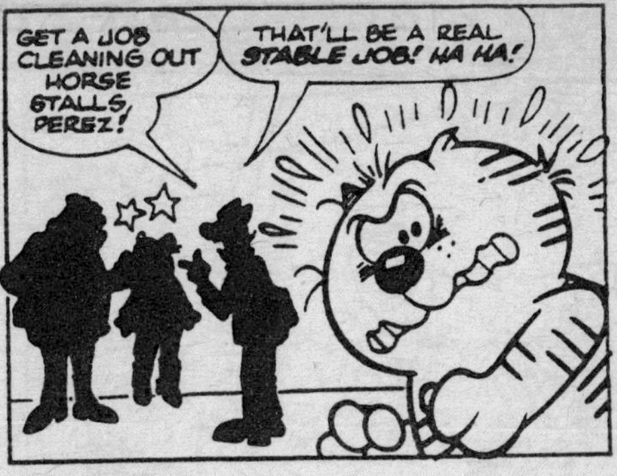
GET A JOB CLEANING OUT HORSE STALLS, PEREZ!
THAT'LL BE A REAL STABLE JOB! HA HA!

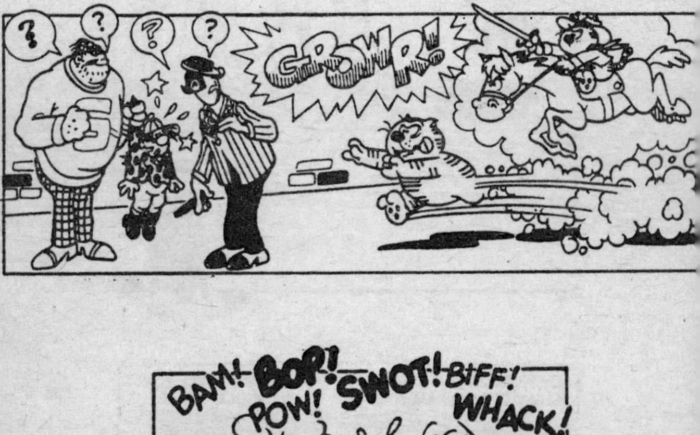
?
?
?
?
CROWP!

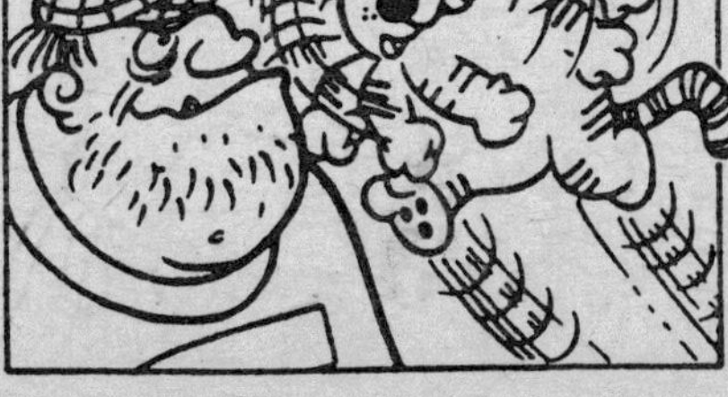
BAM! BOP! POW! SWOT! BIFF! WHACK!

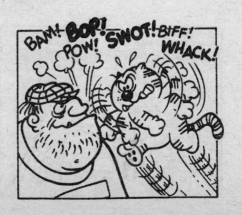

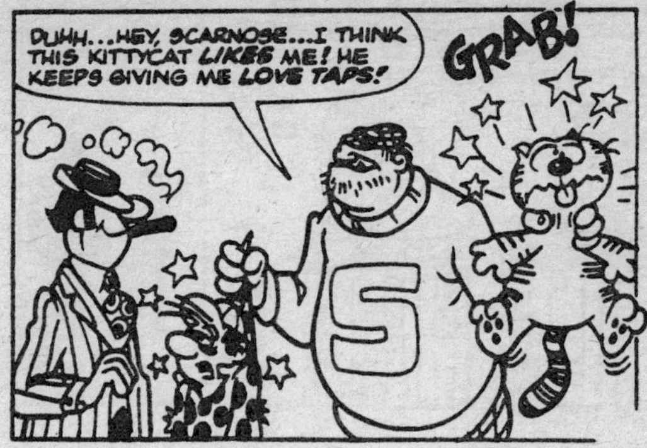
DUHH...HEY, SCARNOSE...I THINK THIS KITTYCAT LIKES ME! HE KEEPS GIVING ME LOVE TAPS!
GRAB!

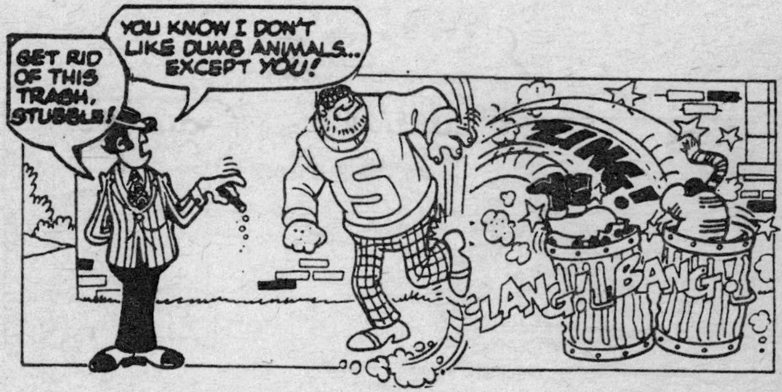
GET RID OF THIS TRASH, STUBBLE!
YOU KNOW I DON'T LIKE DUMB ANIMALS... EXCEPT YOU!
ZING!
CLANG!!
BANG!!

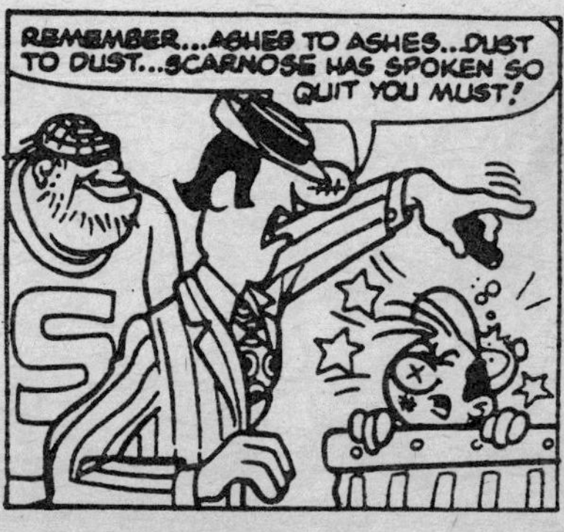
REMEMBER...ASHES TO ASHES...DUST TO DUST...SCARNOSE HAS SPOKEN SO QUIT YOU MUST!

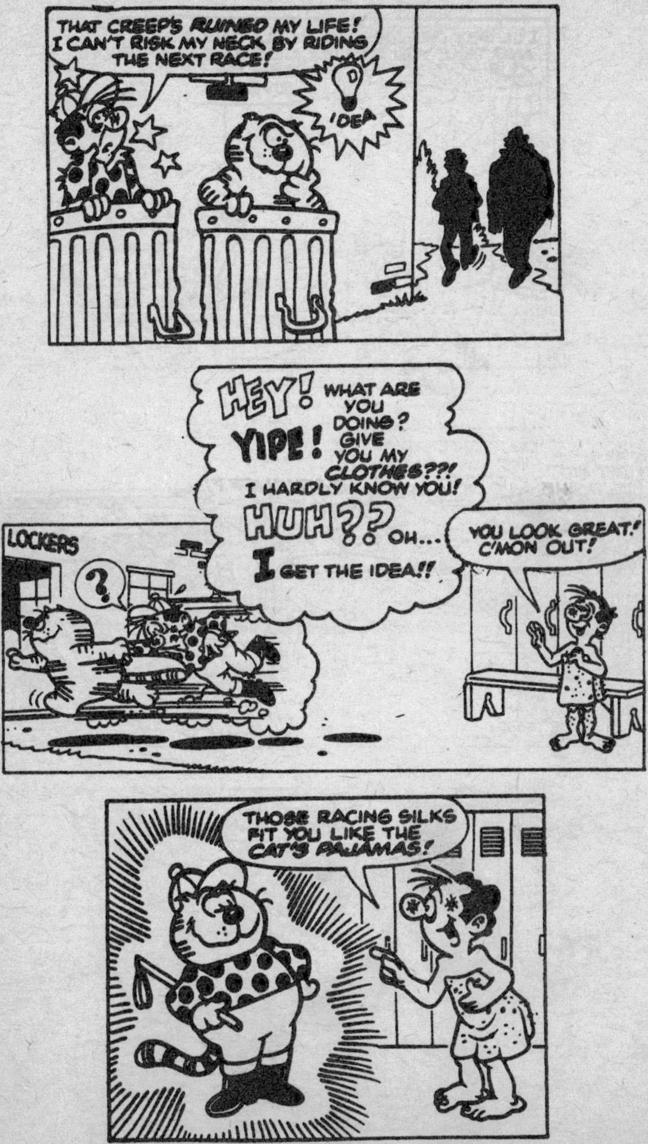

THAT CREEP'S RUINED MY LIFE! I CAN'T RISK MY NECK BY RIDING THE NEXT RACE!
IDEA
HEY! WHAT ARE YOU DOING? YIPE! GIVE YOU MY CLOTHES??! I HARDLY KNOW YOU! HUH?? OH... I GET THE IDEA!!
LOCKERS
?
YOU LOOK GREAT! C'MON OUT!
THOSE RACING SILKS FIT YOU LIKE THE CAT'S PAJAMAS!

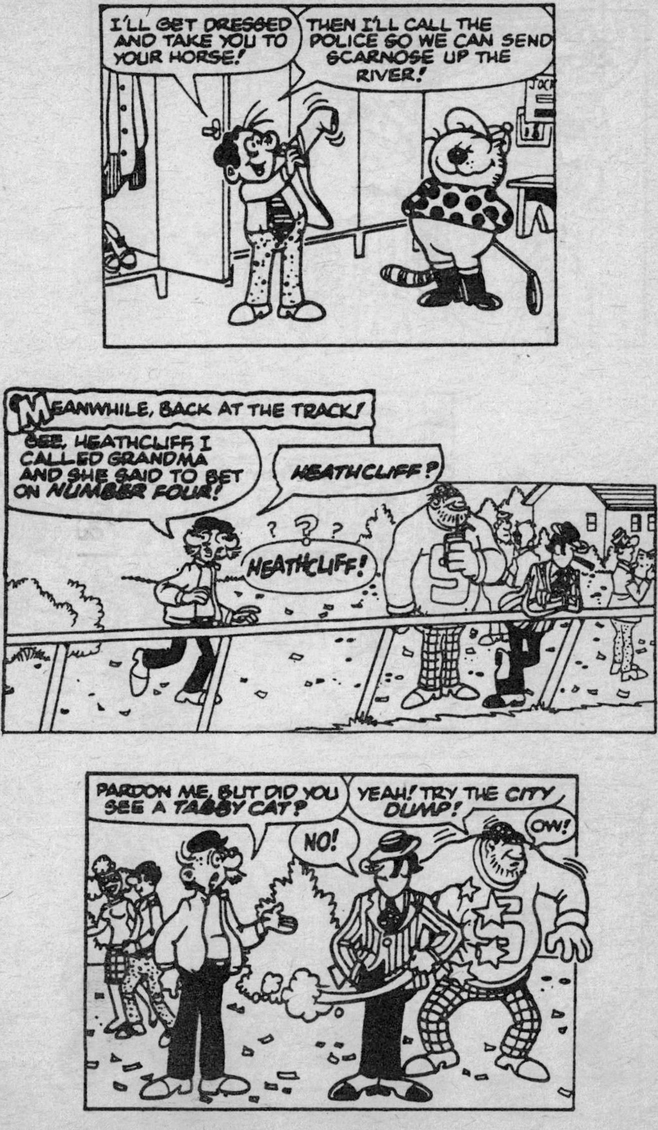
I'LL GET DRESSED AND TAKE YOU TO YOUR HORSE!
THEN I'LL CALL THE POLICE SO WE CAN SEND SCARNOSE UP THE RIVER!
MEANWHILE, BACK AT THE TRACK!
SEE, HEATHCLIFF, I CALLED GRANDMA AND SHE SAID TO BET ON NUMBER FOUR!
HEATHCLIFF?
HEATHCLIFF!
PARDON ME, BUT DID YOU SEE A TABBY CAT?
NO!
YEAH! TRY THE CITY DUMP!
OW!

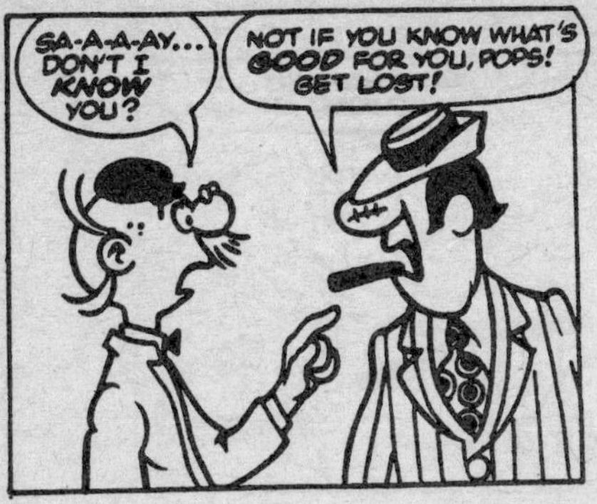
SA-A-A-AY... DON'T I KNOW YOU?
NOT IF YOU KNOW WHAT'S GOOD FOR YOU, POPS! GET LOST!

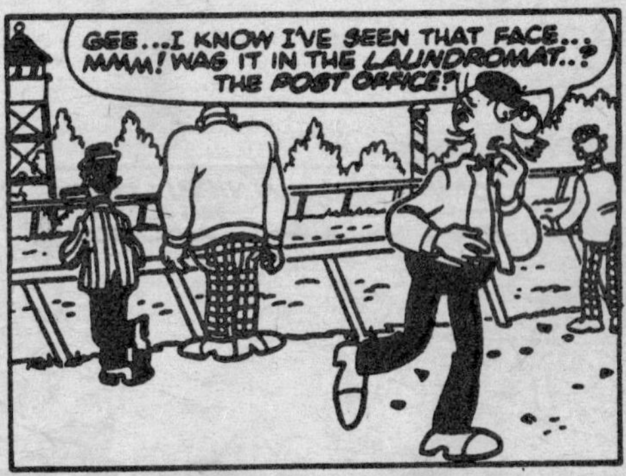
GEE...I KNOW I'VE SEEN THAT FACE... MMM! WAS IT IN THE LAUNDROMAT..? THE POST OFFICE?

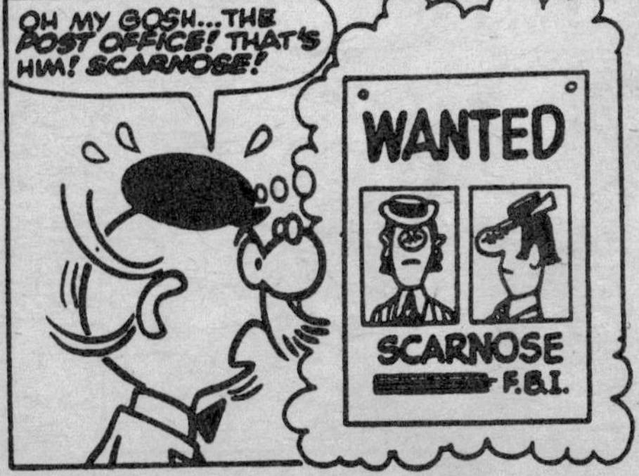
OH MY GOSH...THE POST OFFICE! THAT'S HIM! SCARNOSE!
WANTED
SCARNOSE
F.B.I.

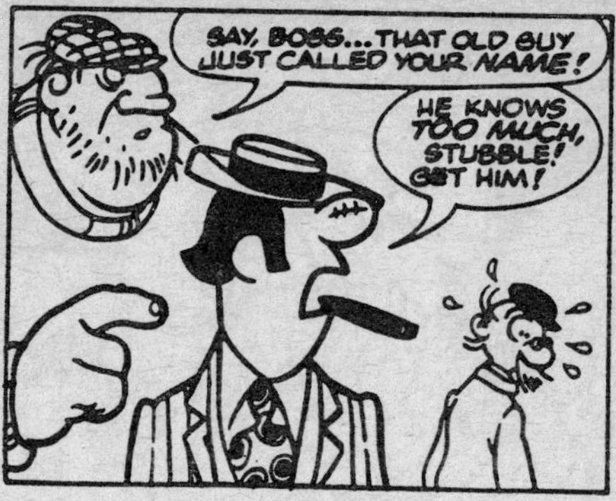
SAY, BOSS...THAT OLD GUY JUST CALLED YOUR NAME!
HE KNOWS TOO MUCH, STUBBLE! GET HIM!

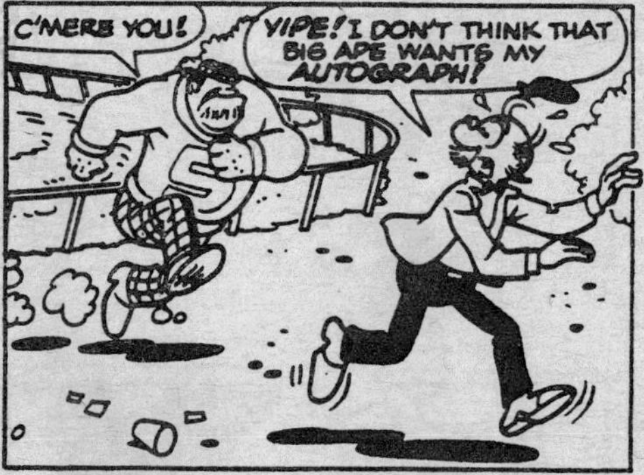
C'MERE YOU!
YIPE! I DON'T THINK THAT BIG APE WANTS MY AUTOGRAPH!

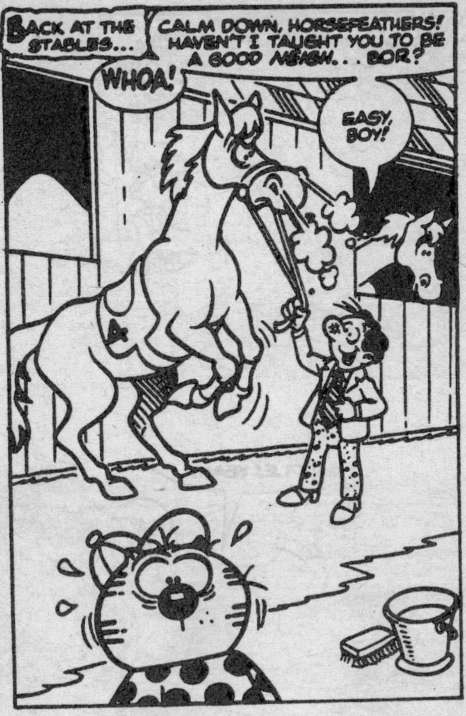
BACK AT THE STABLES...
CALM DOWN, HORSEFEATHERS! HAVEN'T I TAUGHT YOU TO BE A GOOD NEIGH... BOR?
WHOA!
EASY, BOY!

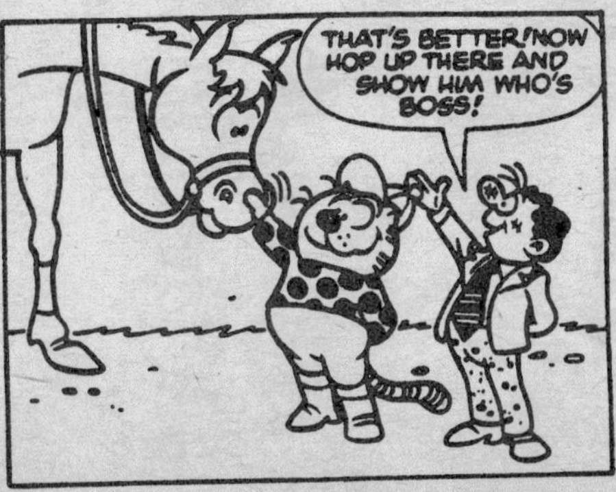
THAT'S BETTER! NOW HOP UP THERE AND SHOW HIM WHO'S BOSS!

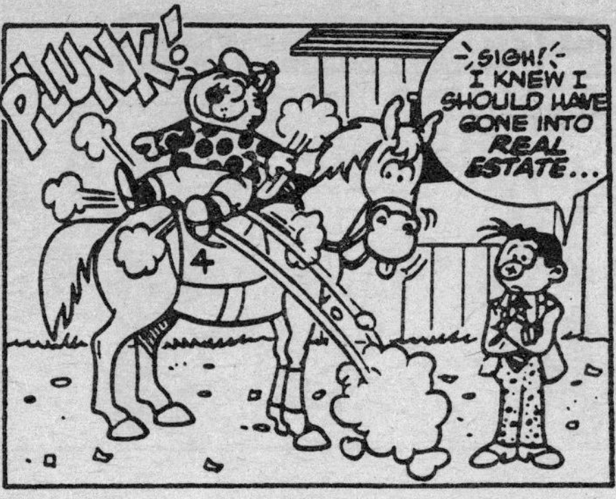
PLUNK!
SIGH! I KNEW I SHOULD HAVE GONE INTO REAL ESTATE...

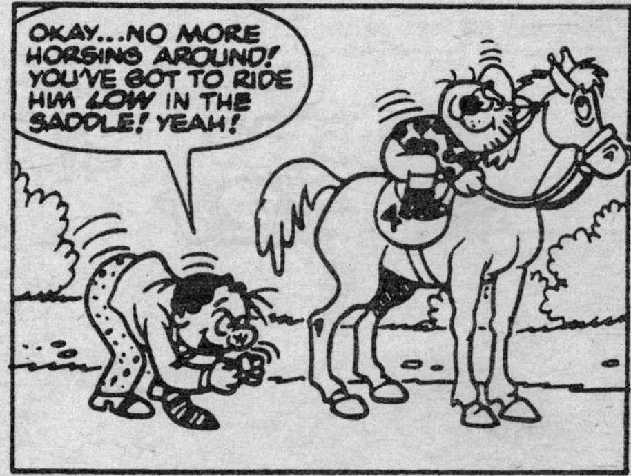
OKAY...NO MORE HORSING AROUND! YOU'VE GOT TO RIDE HIM LOW IN THE SADDLE! YEAH!

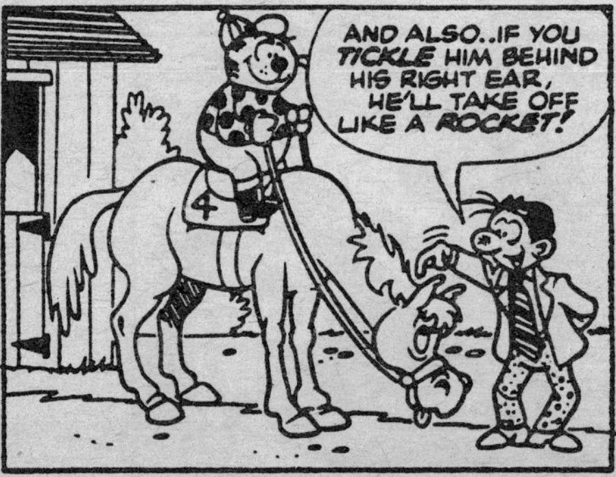
AND ALSO..IF YOU TICKLE HIM BEHIND HIS RIGHT EAR, HE'LL TAKE OFF LIKE A ROCKET!

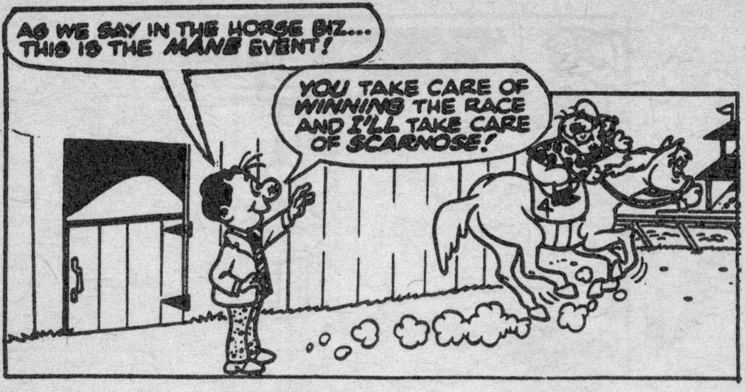
AS WE SAY IN THE HORSE BIZ... THIS IS THE MANE EVENT!
YOU TAKE CARE OF WINNING THE RACE AND I'LL TAKE CARE OF SCARNOSE!
4

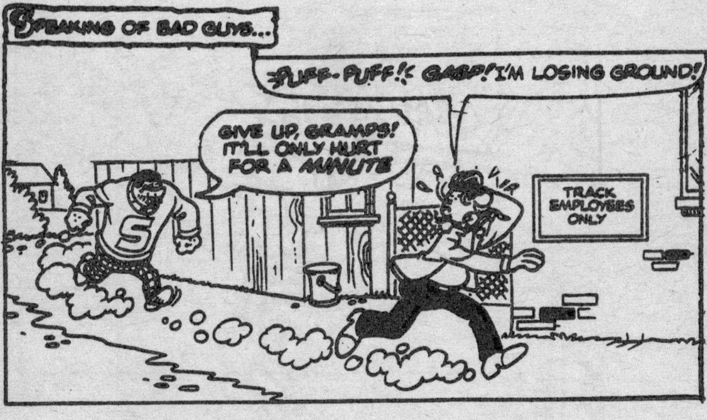
SPEAKING OF BAD GUYS...
PUFF-PUFF! GASP! I'M LOSING GROUND!
GIVE UP, GRAMPS! IT'LL ONLY HURT FOR A MINUTE
S
TRACK EMPLOYEES ONLY

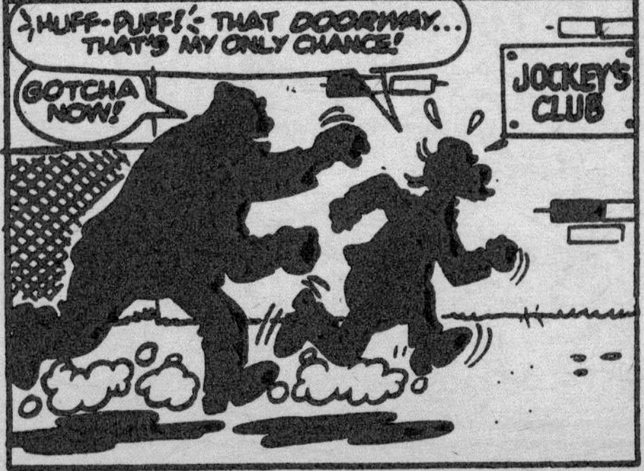
HUFF-PUFF! THAT DOORWAY... THAT'S MY ONLY CHANCE!
GOTCHA NOW!
JOCKEY'S CLUB

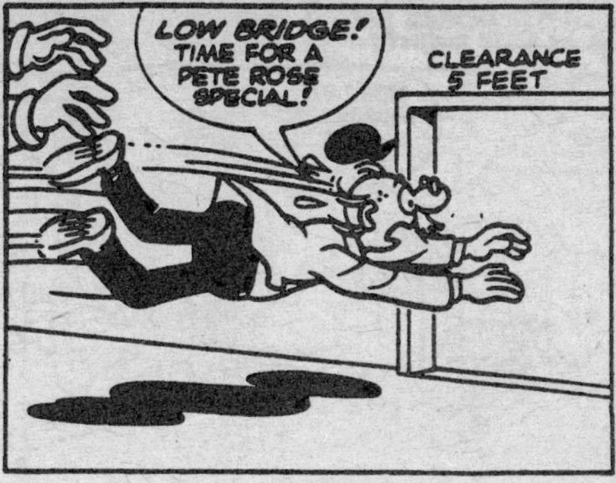
LOW BRIDGE! TIME FOR A PETE ROSE SPECIAL!
CLEARANCE 5 FEET

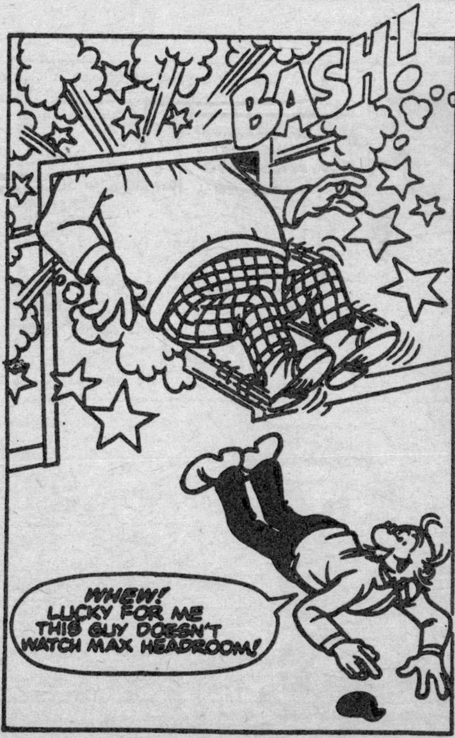
BASH!
WHEW! LUCKY FOR ME THIS GUY DOESN'T WATCH MAX HEADROOM!

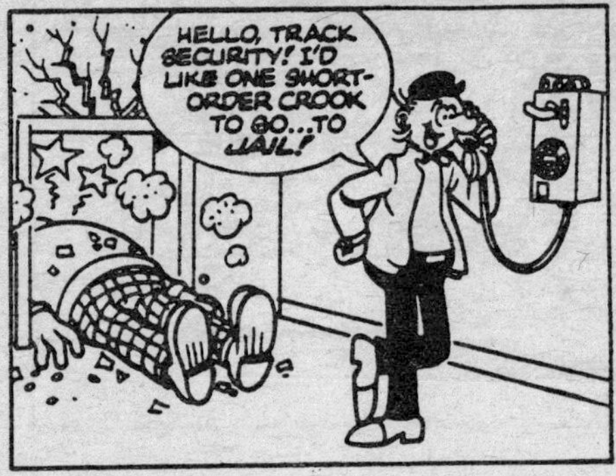
HELLO, TRACK SECURITY! I'D LIKE ONE SHORT-ORDER CROOK TO GO...TO JAIL!

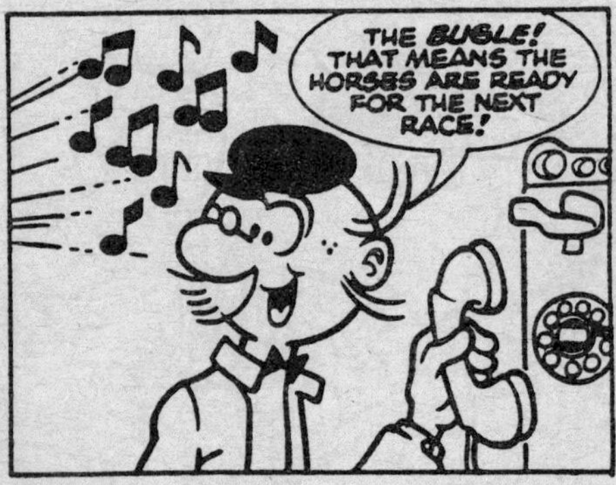
THE BUGLE! THAT MEANS THE HORSES ARE READY FOR THE NEXT RACE!

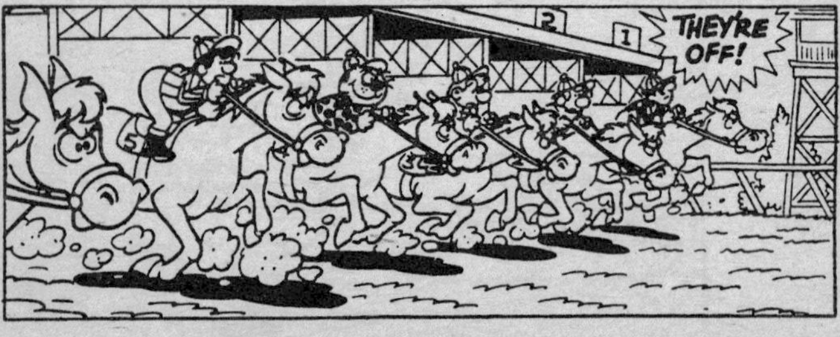
2
1
THEY'RE OFF!

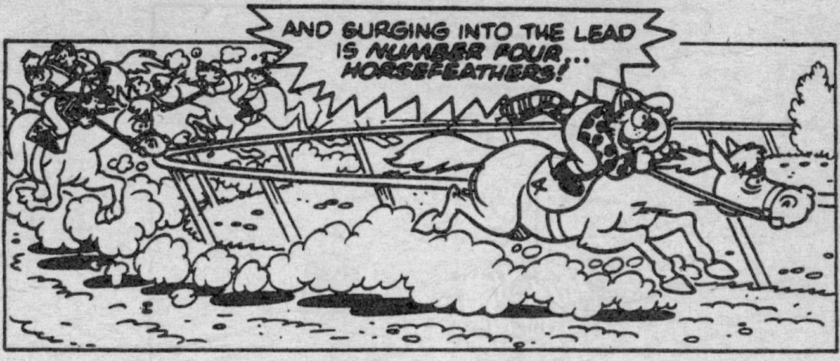
AND SURGING INTO THE LEAD IS NUMBER FOUR... HORSEFEATHERS!

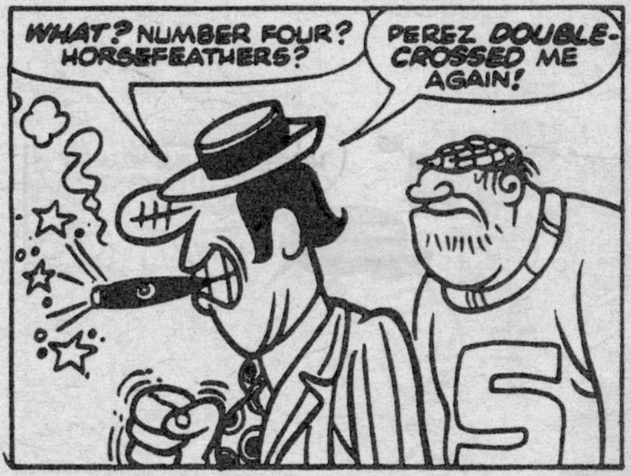
WHAT? NUMBER FOUR? HORSEFEATHERS?
PEREZ DOUBLE-CROSSED ME AGAIN!

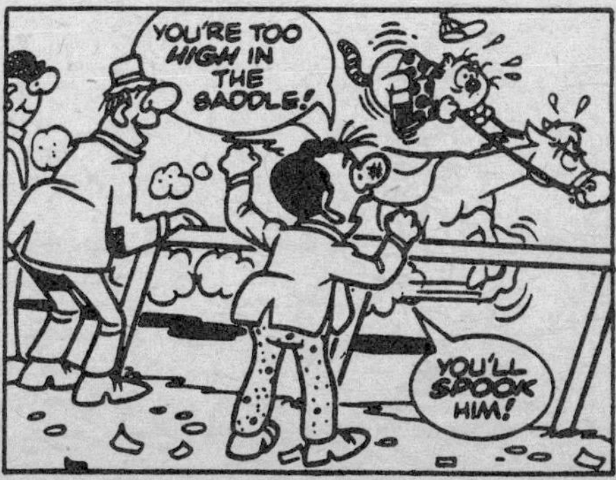
YOU'RE TOO HIGH IN THE SADDLE!
YOU'LL SPOOK HIM!

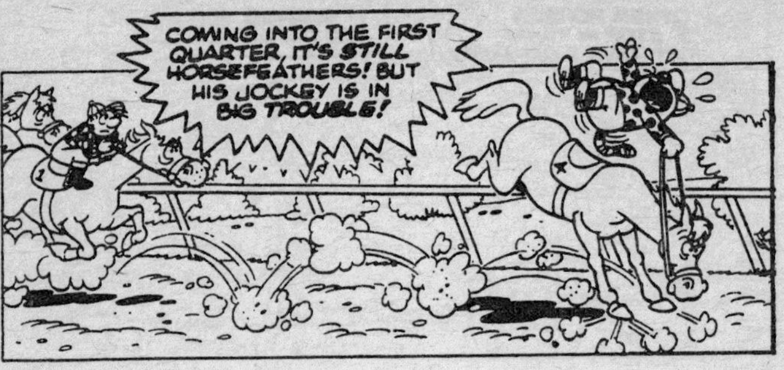
COMING INTO THE FIRST QUARTER, IT'S STILL HORSEFEATHERS! BUT HIS JOCKEY IS IN BIG TROUBLE!

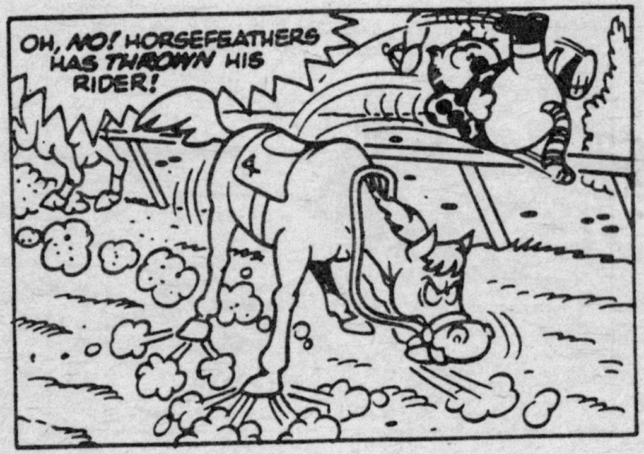
OH, NO! HORSEFEATHERS HAS THROWN HIS RIDER!

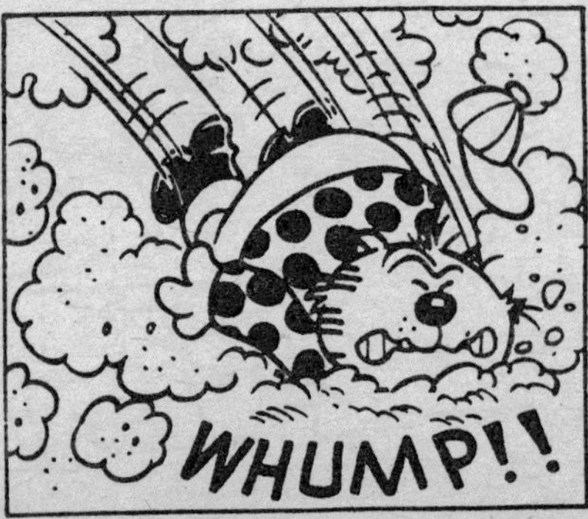
WHUMP!!

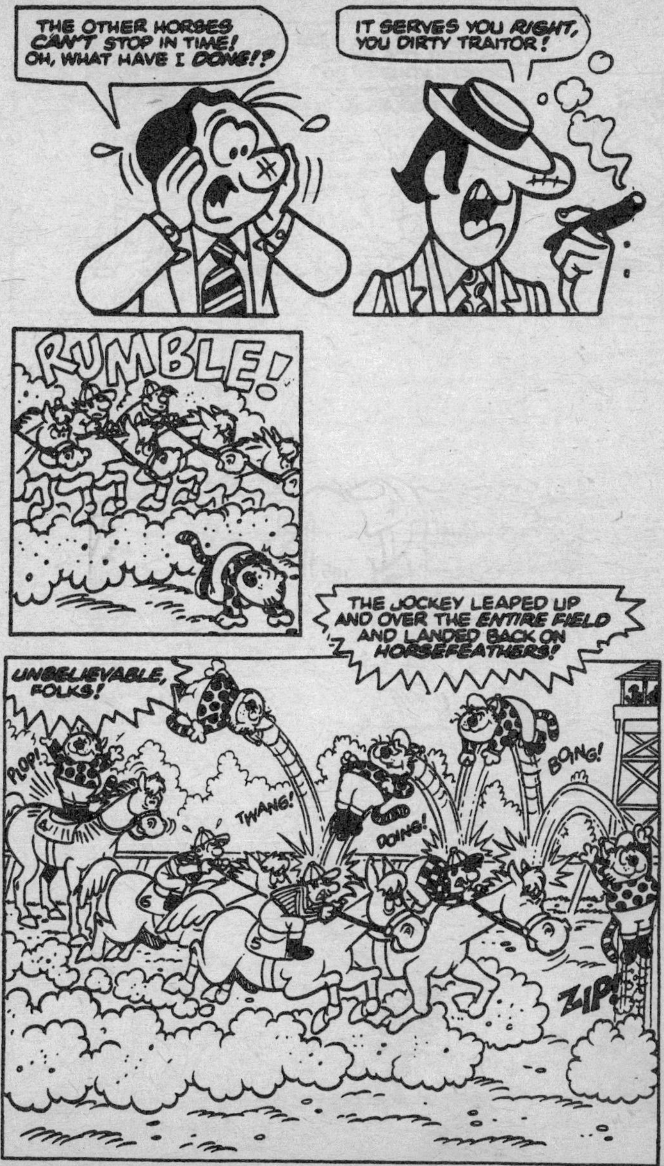
THE OTHER HORSES CAN'T STOP IN TIME! OH, WHAT HAVE I DONE!?
IT SERVES YOU RIGHT, YOU DIRTY TRAITOR!
RUMBLE!
THE JOCKEY LEAPED UP AND OVER THE ENTIRE FIELD AND LANDED BACK ON HORSEFEATHERS!
UNBELIEVABLE, FOLKS!
PLOP!
TWANG!
DOING!
BOING!
ZIP!

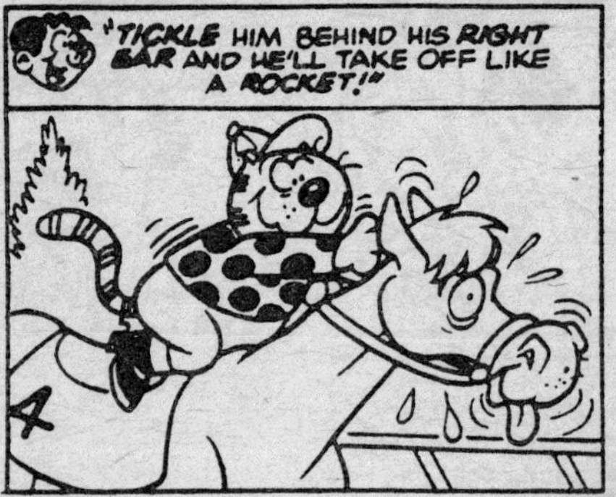
"TICKLE HIM BEHIND HIS RIGHT EAR AND HE'LL TAKE OFF LIKE A ROCKET!"
4

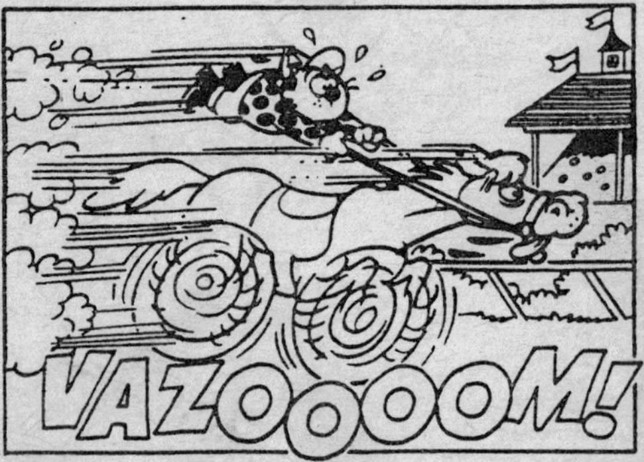
VAZOOOOOM!

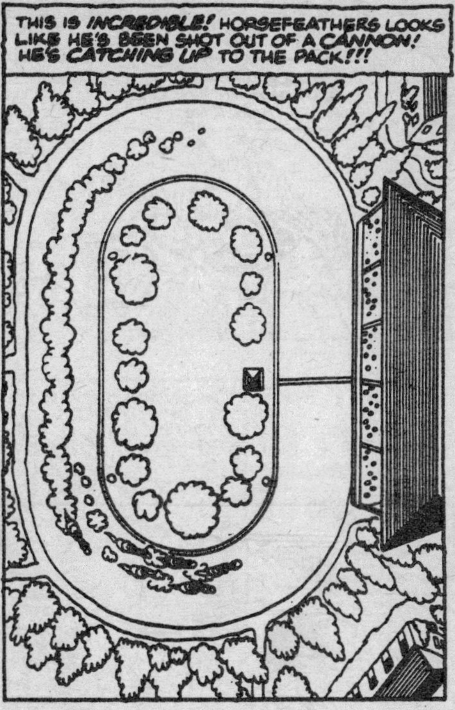
THIS IS INCREDIBLE! HORSEFEATHERS LOOKS LIKE HE'S BEEN SHOT OUT OF A CANNON! HE'S CATCHING UP TO THE PACK!!!

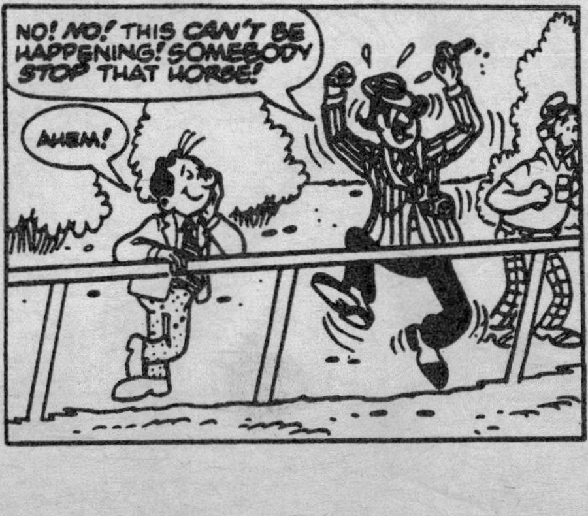
NO! NO! THIS CAN'T BE HAPPENING! SOMEBODY STOP THAT HORSE!
AHEM!

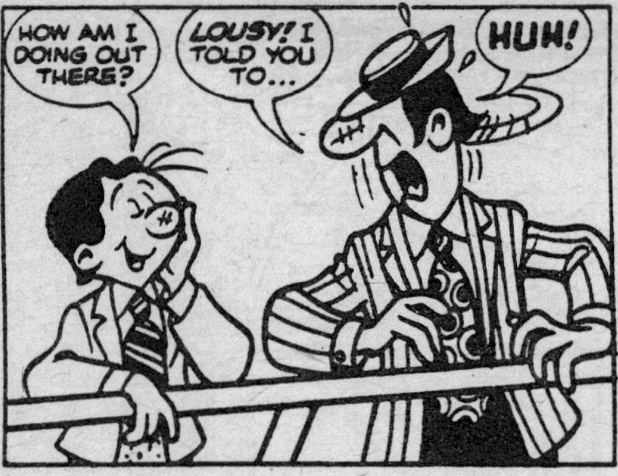
HOW AM I DOING OUT THERE?
LOUSY! I TOLD YOU TO...
HUH!

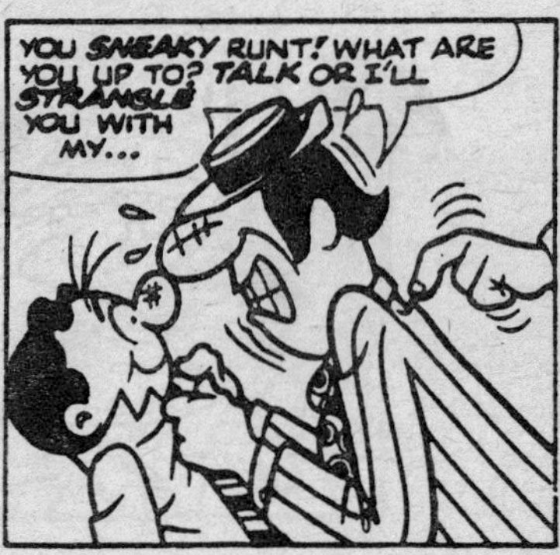
YOU SNEAKY RUNT! WHAT ARE YOU UP TO? TALK OR I'LL STRANGLE YOU WITH MY...

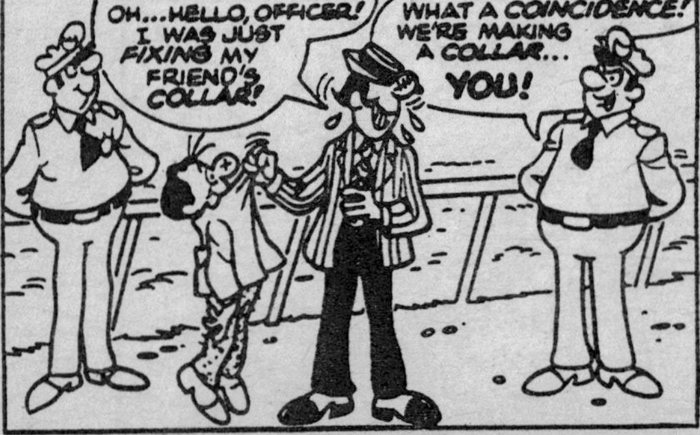
OH...HELLO, OFFICER! I WAS JUST FIXING MY FRIEND'S COLLAR!
WHAT A COINCIDENCE! WE'RE MAKING A COLLAR... YOU!

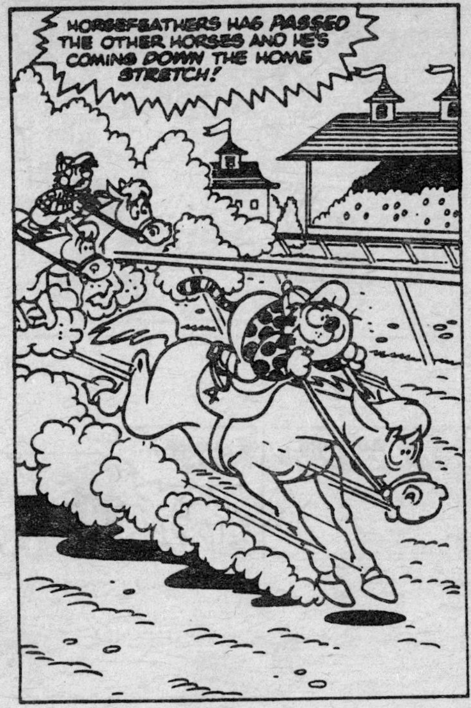
HORSEFEATHERS HAS PASSED THE OTHER HORSES AND HE'S COMING DOWN THE HOME STRETCH!

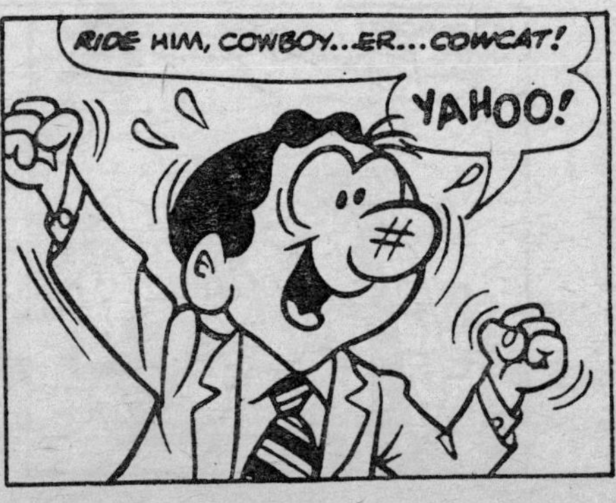
RIDE HIM, COWBOY...ER...COWCAT!
YAHOO!

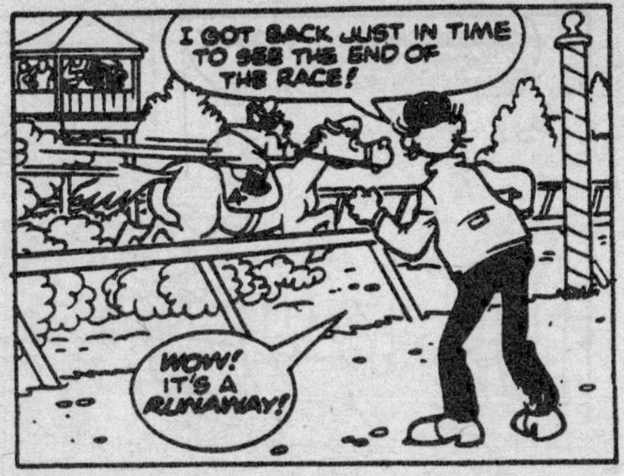
I GOT BACK JUST IN TIME TO SEE THE END OF THE RACE!
WOW! IT'S A RUNAWAY!

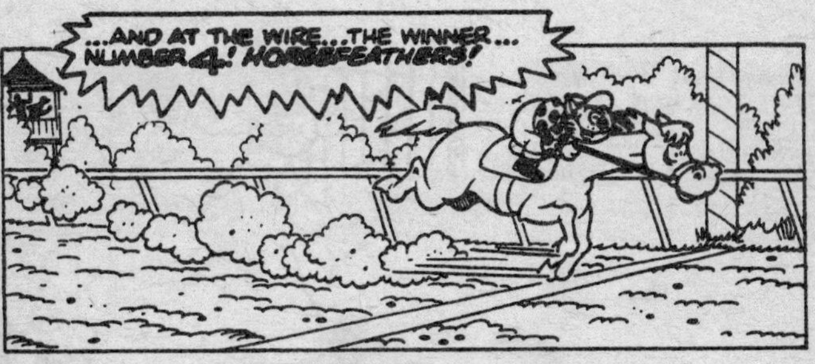
...AND AT THE WIRE...THE WINNER... NUMBER 4! HORSEFEATHERS!

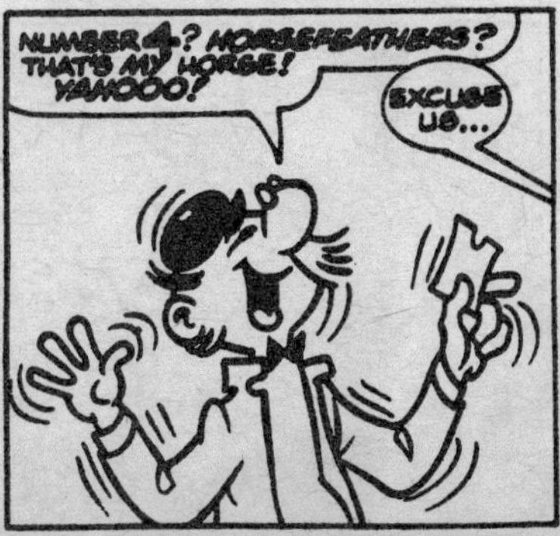
NUMBER 4? HORSEFEATHERS? THAT'S MY HORSE! YAHOOO!
EXCUSE US...

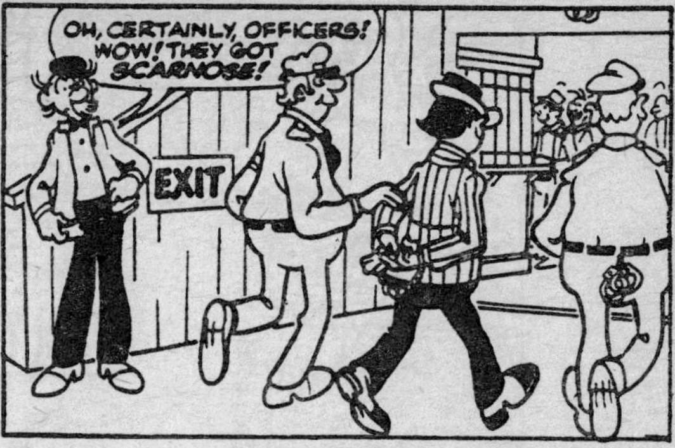
OH, CERTAINLY, OFFICERS! WOW! THEY GOT SCARNOSE!
EXIT

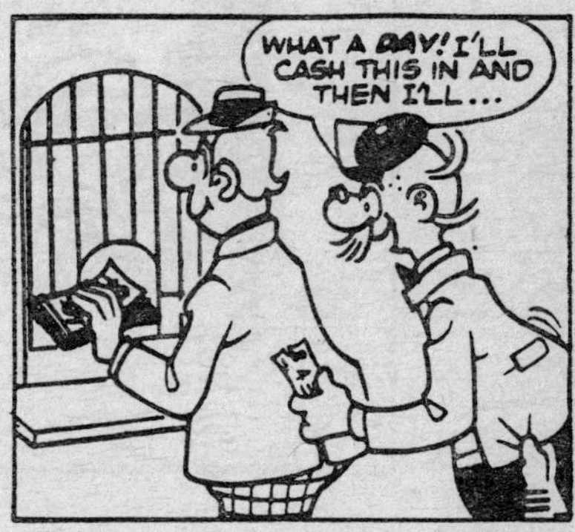
WHAT A DAY! I'LL CASH THIS IN AND THEN I'LL...

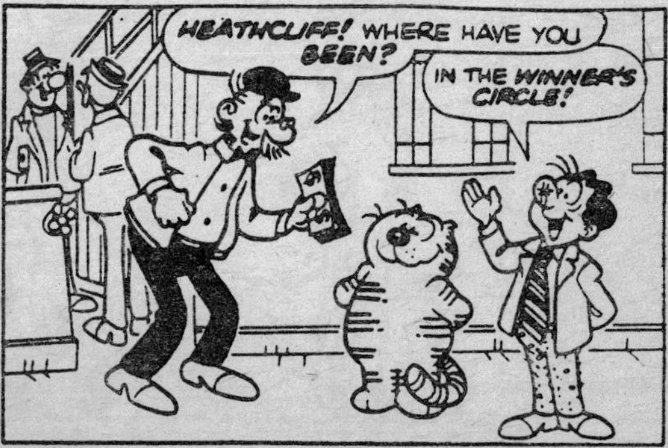
HEATHCLIFF! WHERE HAVE YOU BEEN?
IN THE WINNER'S CIRCLE!

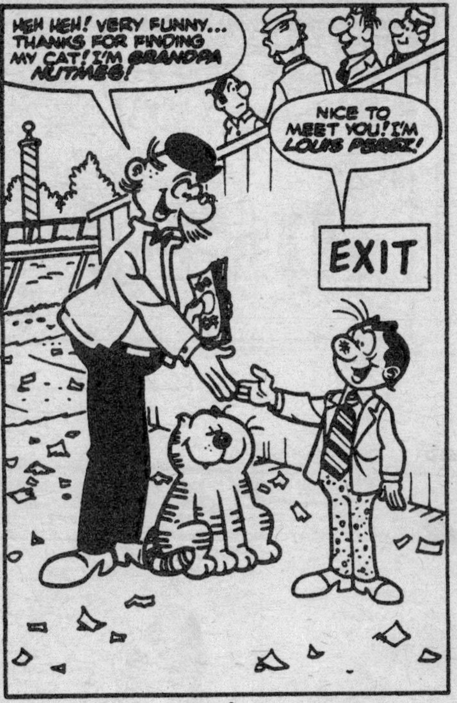
HEH HEH! VERY FUNNY... THANKS FOR FINDING MY CAT! I'M GRANDPA NUTMEG!
NICE TO MEET YOU! I'M LOUIS PEREZ!
EXIT

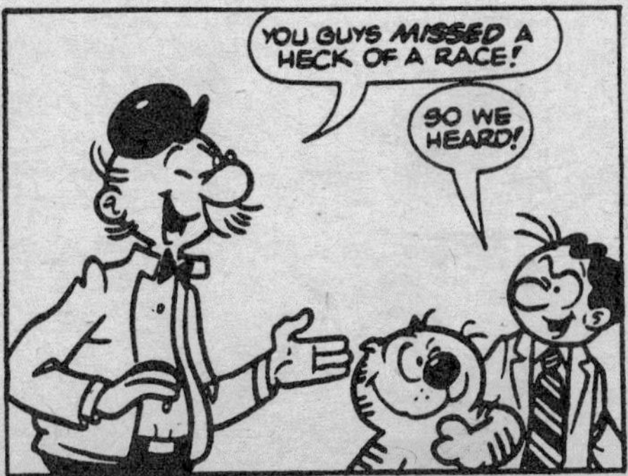
YOU GUYS MISSED A HECK OF A RACE!
SO WE HEARD!

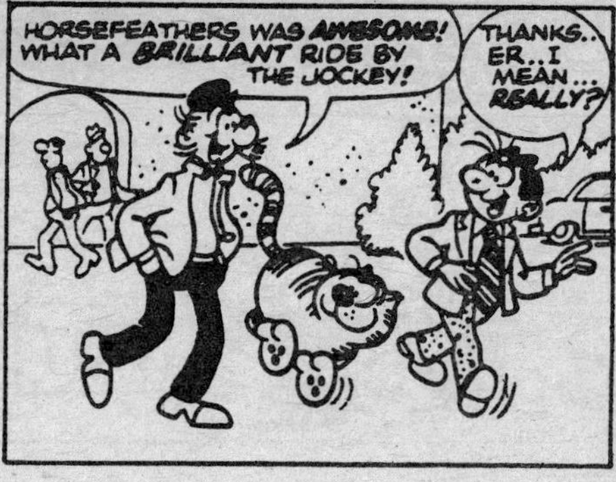
HORSEFEATHERS WAS AWESOME! WHAT A BRILLIANT RIDE BY THE JOCKEY!
THANKS.. ER..I MEAN... REALLY?

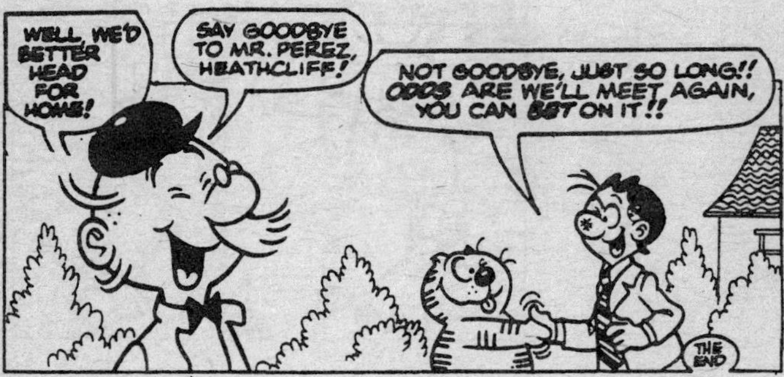
WELL, WE'D BETTER HEAD FOR HOME!
SAY GOODBYE TO MR. PEREZ, HEATHCLIFF!
NOT GOODBYE, JUST SO LONG!! ODDS ARE WE'LL MEET AGAIN, YOU CAN BET ON IT!!
THE END

AT THE RAT

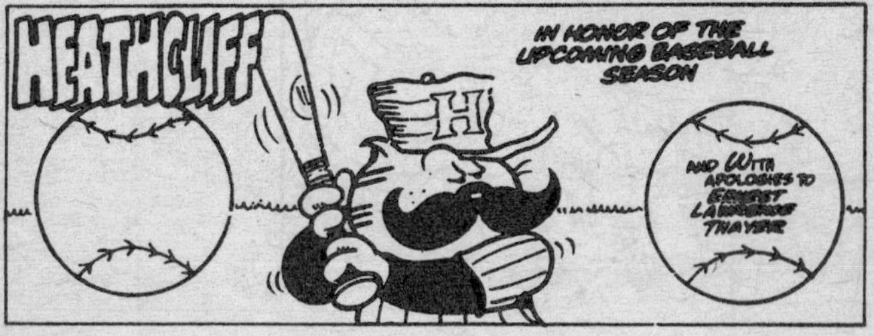
HEATHCLIFF
IN HONOR OF THE UPCOMING BASEBALL SEASON
AND WITH APOLOGIES TO ERNEST LAWRENCE THAYER

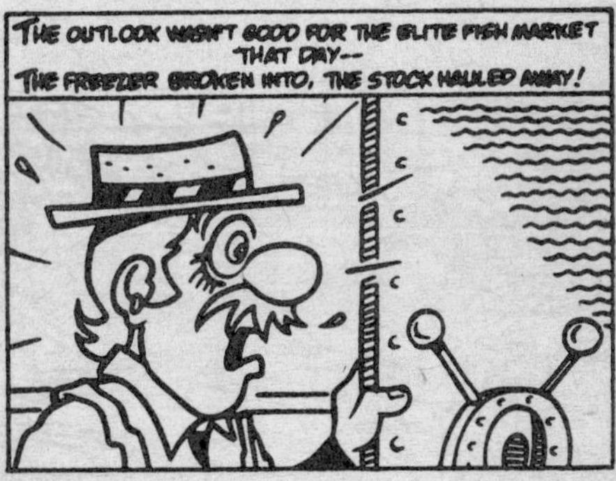
THE OUTLOOK WASN'T GOOD FOR THE ELITE FISH MARKET THAT DAY--
THE FREEZER BROKEN INTO, THE STOCK HAULED AWAY!

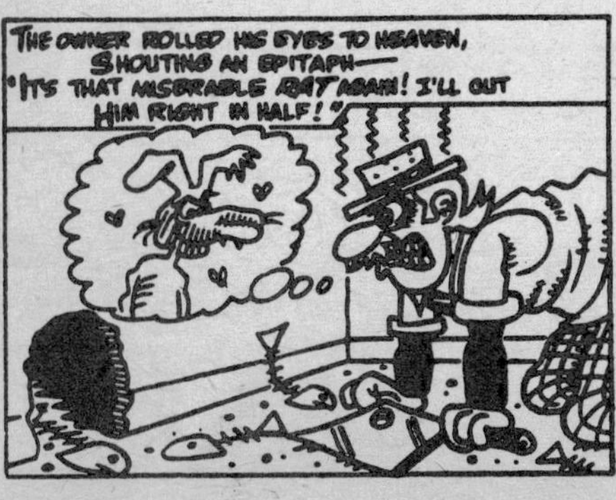
THE OWNER ROLLED HIS EYES TO HEAVEN, SHOUTING AN EPITAPH—
"IT'S THAT MISERABLE RAT AGAIN! I'LL CUT HIM RIGHT IN HALF!"

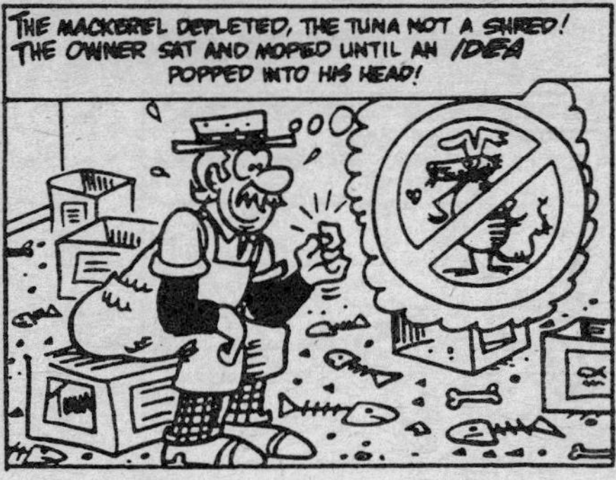
THE MACKEREL DEPLETED, THE TUNA NOT A SHRED! THE OWNER SAT AND MOPED UNTIL AN IDEA POPPED INTO HIS HEAD!

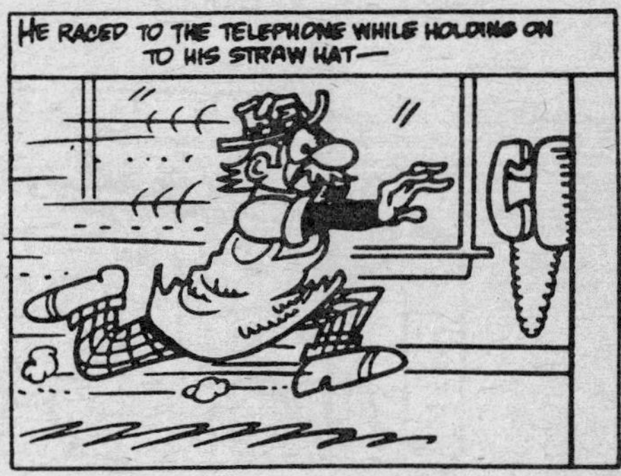
HE RACED TO THE TELEPHONE WHILE HOLDING ON TO HIS STRAW HAT—

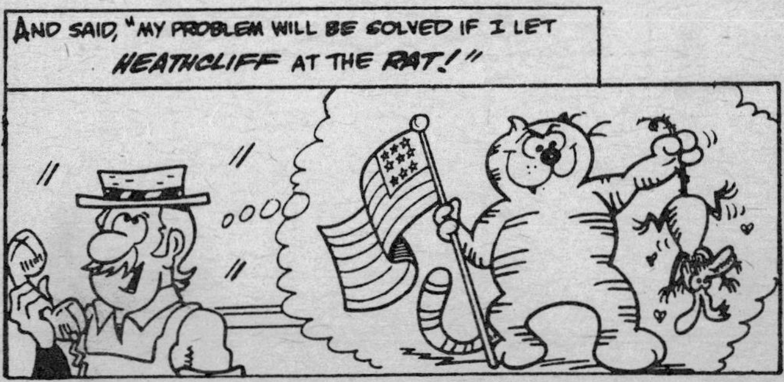
AND SAID, "MY PROBLEM WILL BE SOLVED IF I LET HEATHCLIFF AT THE RAT!"

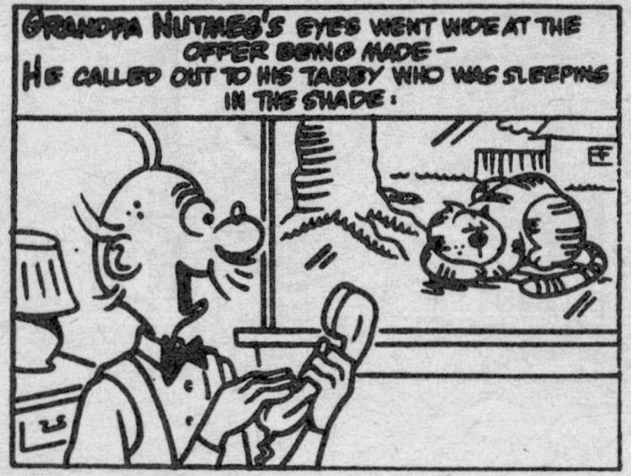
GRANDPA NUTMEG'S EYES WENT WIDE AT THE OFFER BEING MADE—
HE CALLED OUT TO HIS TABBY WHO WAS SLEEPING IN THE SHADE:

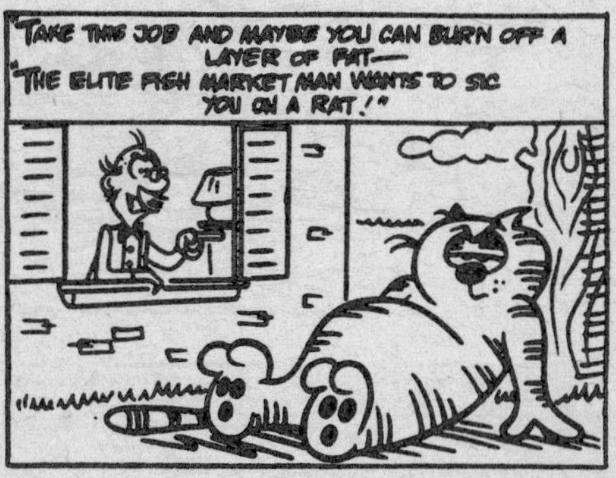
"TAKE THIS JOB AND MAYBE YOU CAN BURN OFF A LAYER OF FAT—
"THE ELITE FISH MARKET MAN WANTS TO SIC YOU ON A RAT!"

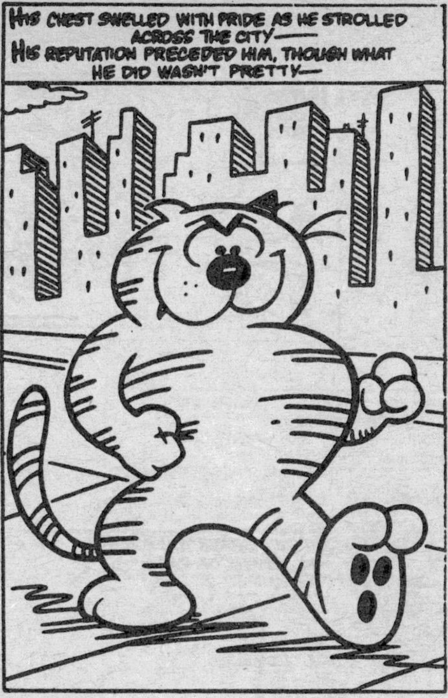
HIS CHEST SWELLED WITH PRIDE AS HE STROLLED ACROSS THE CITY—
HIS REPUTATION PRECEDED HIM, THOUGH WHAT HE DID WASN'T PRETTY—

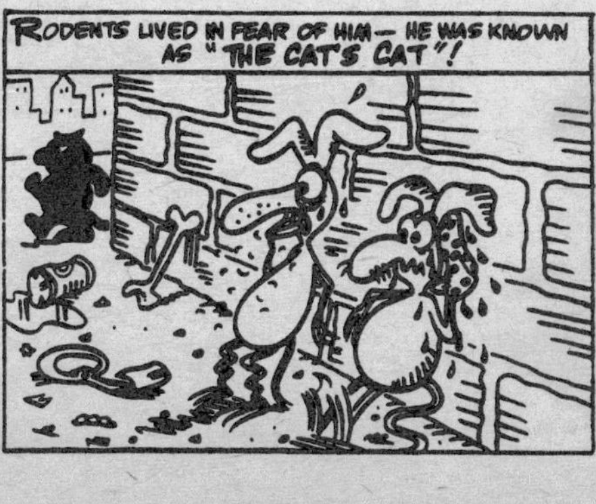
RODENTS LIVED IN FEAR OF HIM— HE WAS KNOWN AS "THE CAT'S CAT"!

IT WAS ONLY LOGICAL TO SEND *HEATHCLIFF* AFTER THE RAT!

HEIGHT
WEIGHT
REACH
WON
LOST
KO's

A NOISY CROWD HAD GATHERED OUTSIDE THE ELITE FISH STORE, THEY KNEW THAT HEATHCLIFF WOULD GIVE THE THIEVING RAT "WHAT FOR"!

Elite

THE OWNER USHERED HIM INSIDE AND GAVE HIM A BASEBALL BAT— HE SHOWED HIM THE EVIDENCE AND TOLD HEATHCLIFF TO WHIP THE RAT!

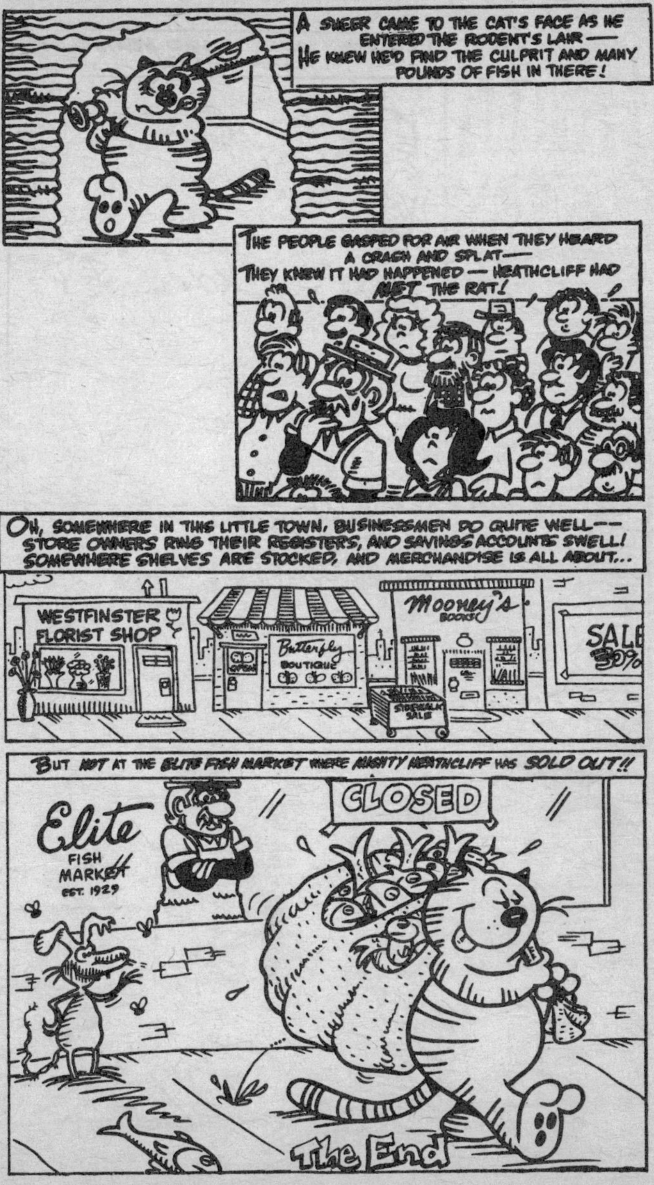
A SNEER CAME TO THE CAT'S FACE AS HE ENTERED THE RODENT'S LAIR—
HE KNEW HE'D FIND THE CULPRIT AND MANY POUNDS OF FISH IN THERE!
THE PEOPLE GASPED FOR AIR WHEN THEY HEARD A CRASH AND SPLAT—
THEY KNEW IT HAD HAPPENED — HEATHCLIFF HAD MET THE RAT!
OH, SOMEWHERE IN THIS LITTLE TOWN, BUSINESSMEN DO QUITE WELL—
STORE OWNERS RING THEIR REGISTERS, AND SAVINGS ACCOUNTS SWELL!
SOMEWHERE SHELVES ARE STOCKED, AND MERCHANDISE IS ALL ABOUT...
WESTFINSTER FLORIST SHOP
OPEN
Butterfly BOUTIQUE
Mooney's BOOKS
SIDEWALK SALE
SALE 30%
BUT NOT AT THE ELITE FISH MARKET WHERE MIGHTY HEATHCLIFF HAS SOLD OUT!!
CLOSED
Elite FISH MARKET EST. 1929
The End

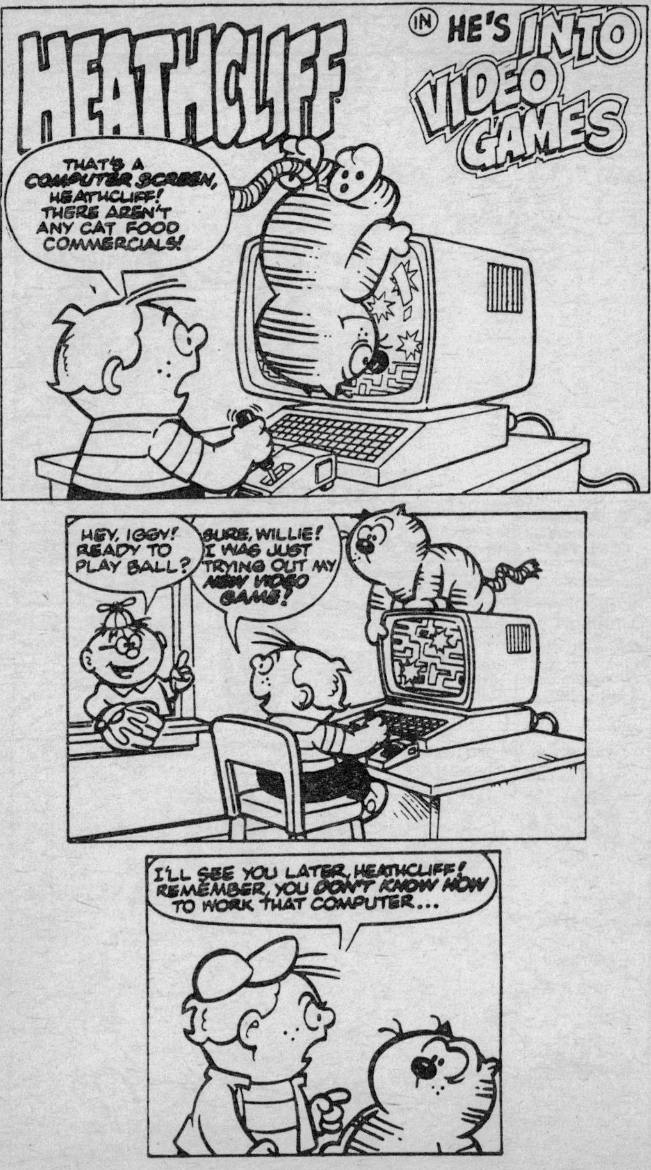
HEATHCLIFF
IN HE'S INTO VIDEO GAMES
THAT'S A COMPUTER SCREEN, HEATHCLIFF! THERE AREN'T ANY CAT FOOD COMMERCIALS!
HEY, IGGY! READY TO PLAY BALL?
SURE, WILLIE! I WAS JUST TRYING OUT MY NEW VIDEO GAME!
I'LL SEE YOU LATER, HEATHCLIFF! REMEMBER, YOU DON'T KNOW HOW TO WORK THAT COMPUTER...

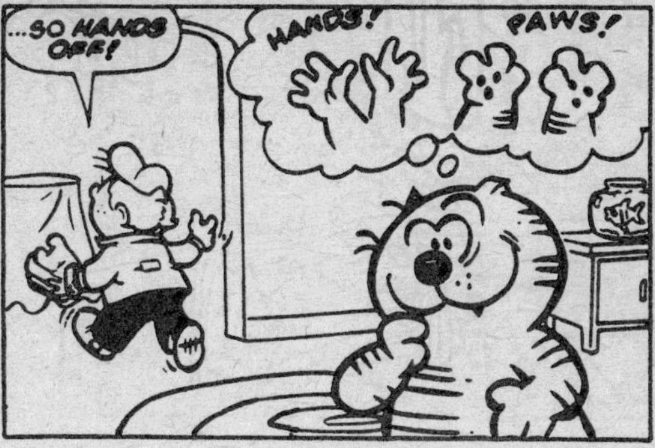
...SO HANDS OFF!
HANDS! PAWS!

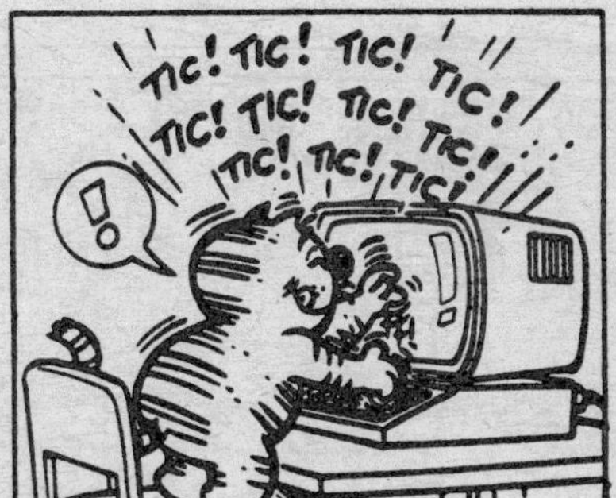
TIC! TIC! TIC! TIC! TIC! TIC! TIC! TIC! TIC! TIC! TIC!
!

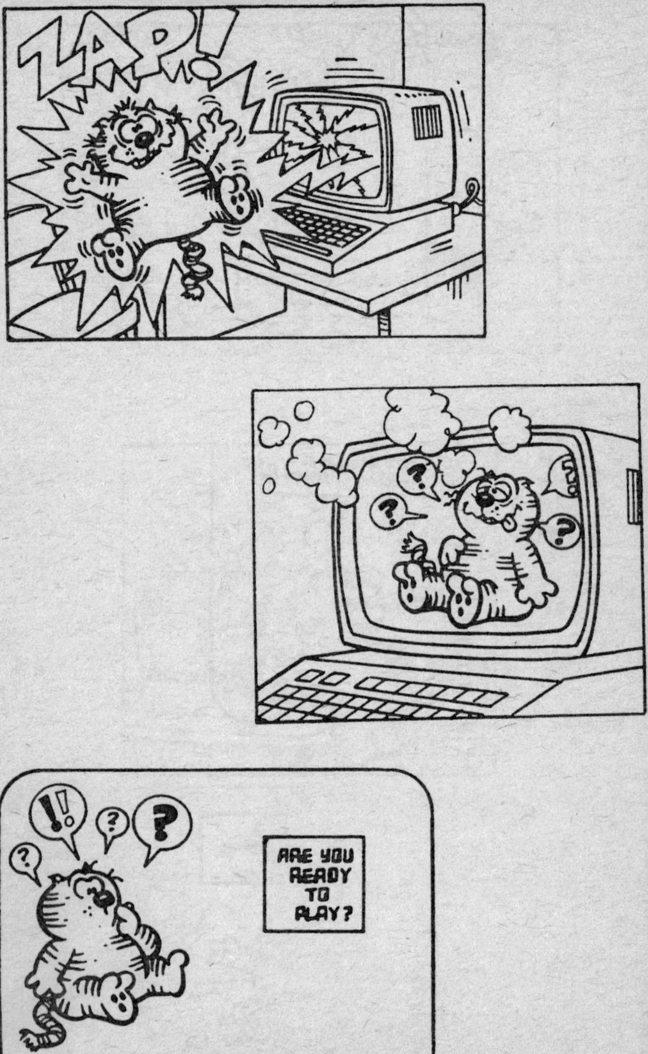
ZAP!
ARE YOU READY TO PLAY?

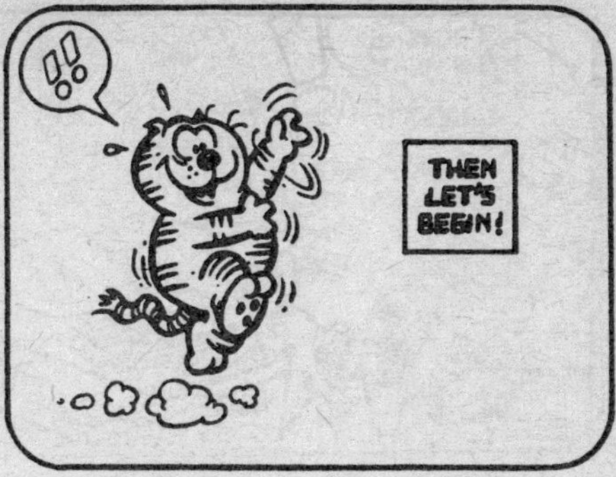
!!
THEN LET'S BEGIN!

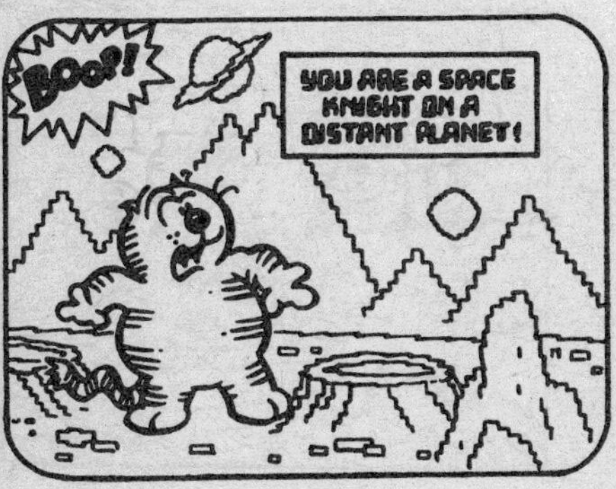
BOOP!
YOU ARE A SPACE KNIGHT ON A DISTANT PLANET!

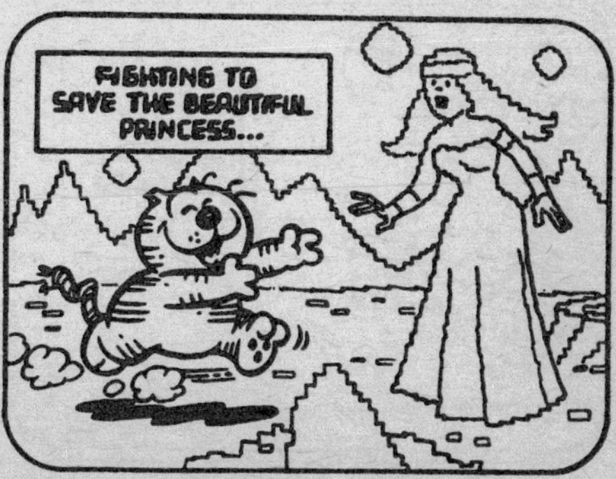
FIGHTING TO SAVE THE BEAUTIFUL PRINCESS...

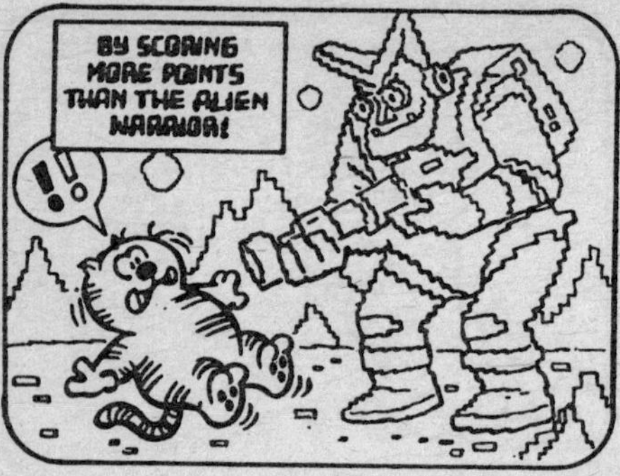
BY SCORING MORE POINTS THAN THE ALIEN WARRIOR!
!!

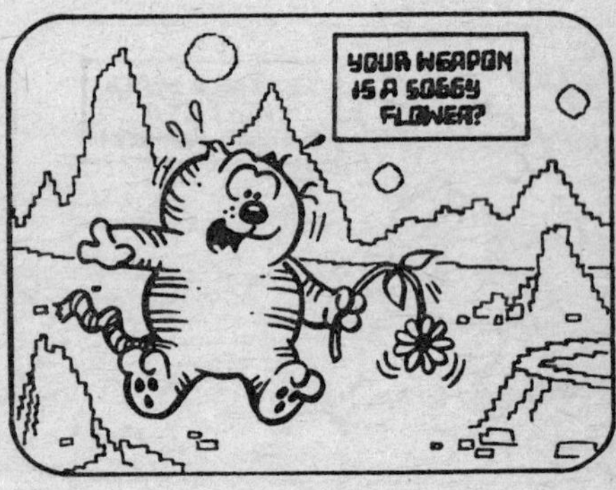
YOUR WEAPON IS A SOGGY FLOWER?

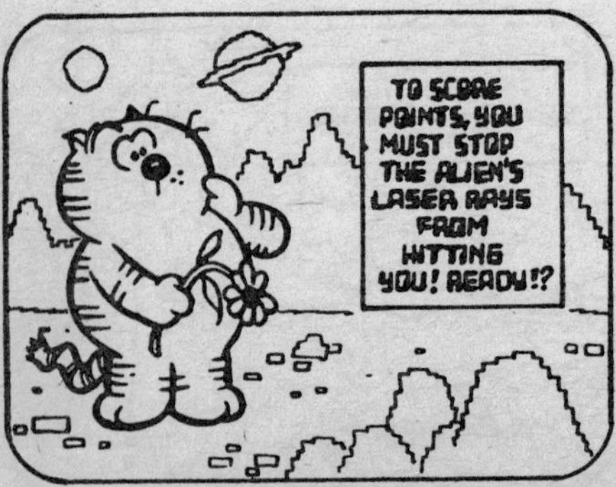
TO SCORE POINTS, YOU MUST STOP THE ALIEN'S LASER RAYS FROM HITTING YOU! READY!?

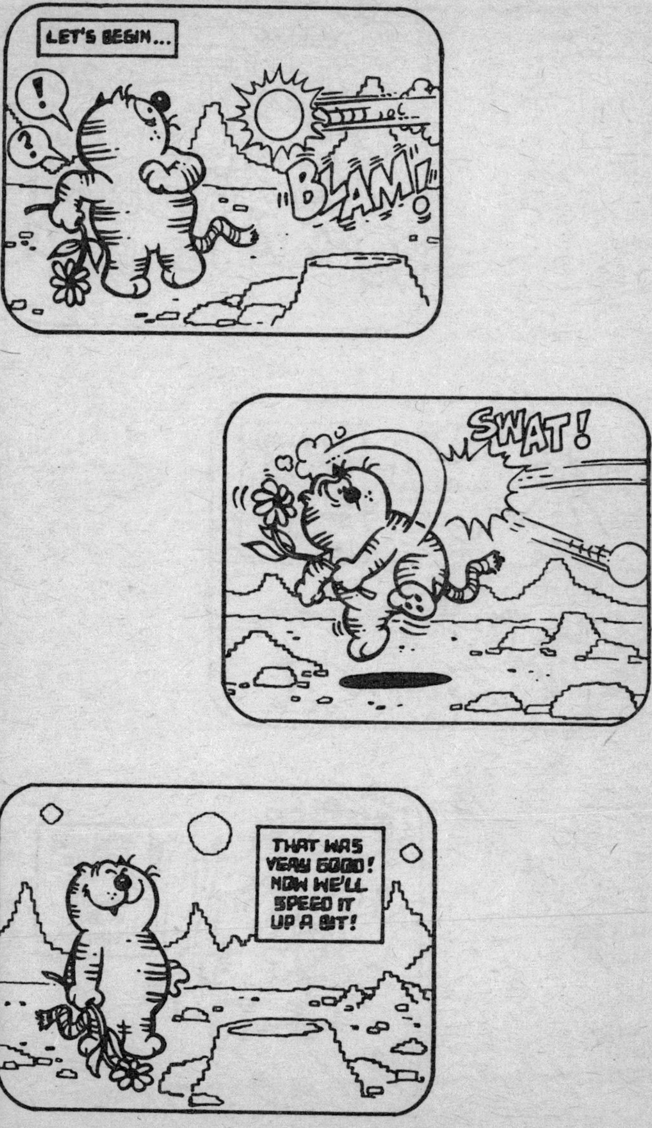
LET'S BEGIN...
!
?
BLAM!
SWAT!
THAT WAS VERY GOOD! NOW WE'LL SPEED IT UP A BIT!

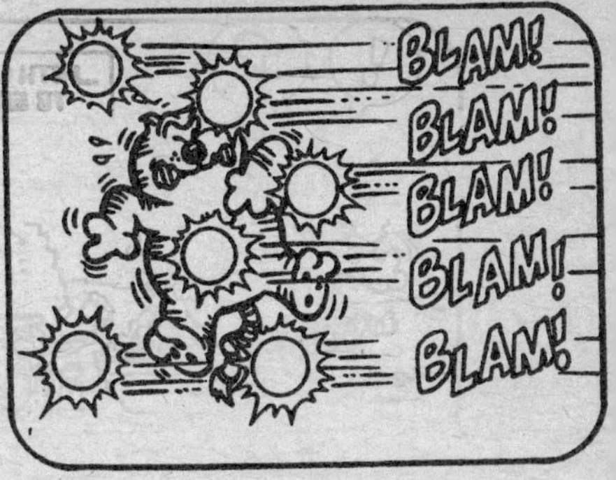
BLAM!
BLAM!
BLAM!
BLAM!
BLAM!

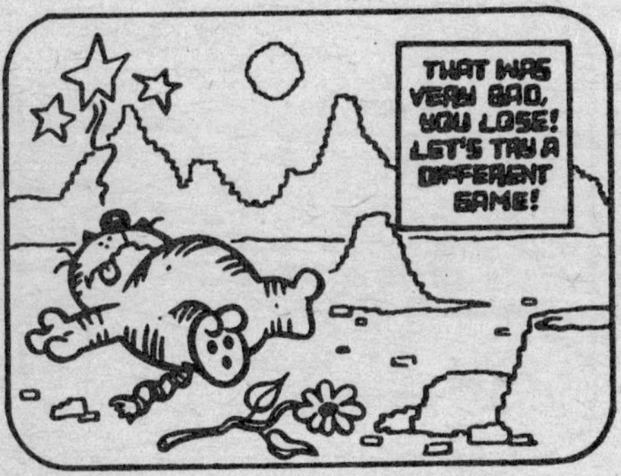
THAT WAS VERY BAD, YOU LOSE! LET'S TRY A DIFFERENT GAME!

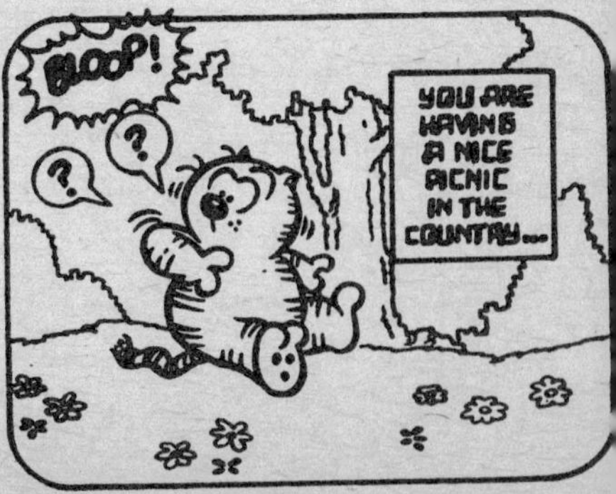
BLOOP!
?
?
YOU ARE HAVING A NICE PICNIC IN THE COUNTRY...

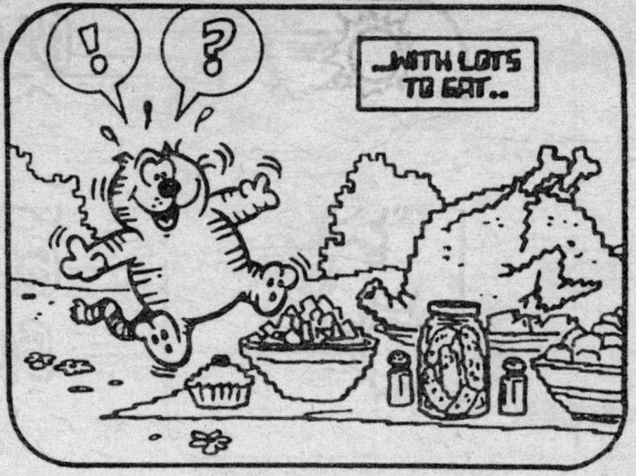
!
?
..WITH LOTS TO EAT..

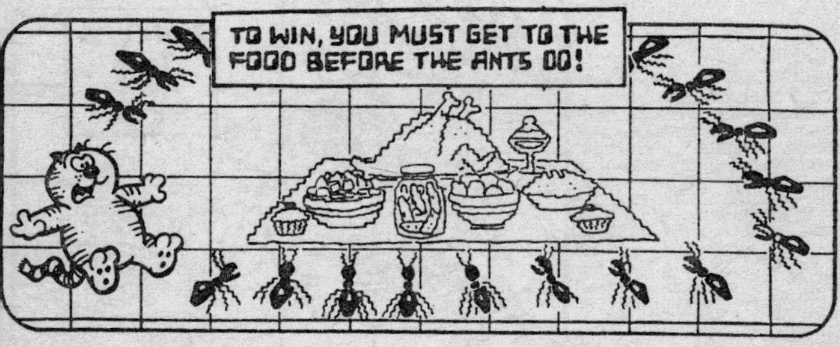
TO WIN, YOU MUST GET TO THE FOOD BEFORE THE ANTS DO!

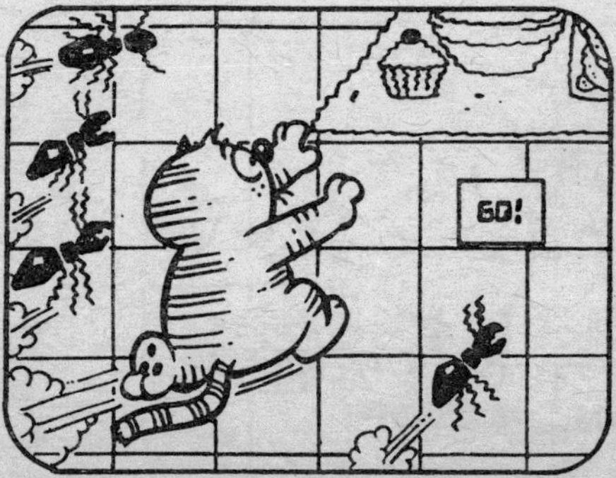
GO!

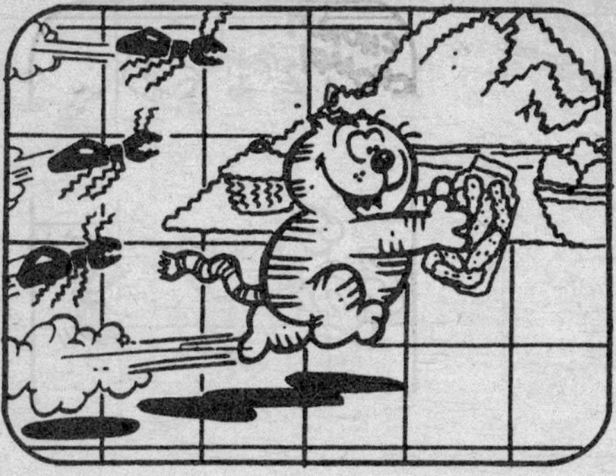

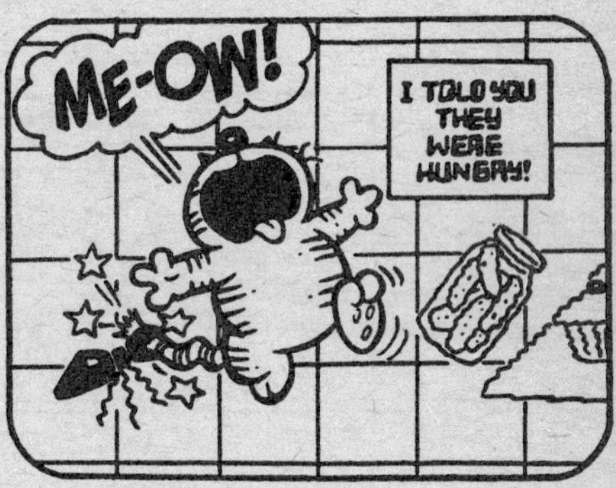
ME-OW!
I TOLD YOU THEY WERE HUNGRY!

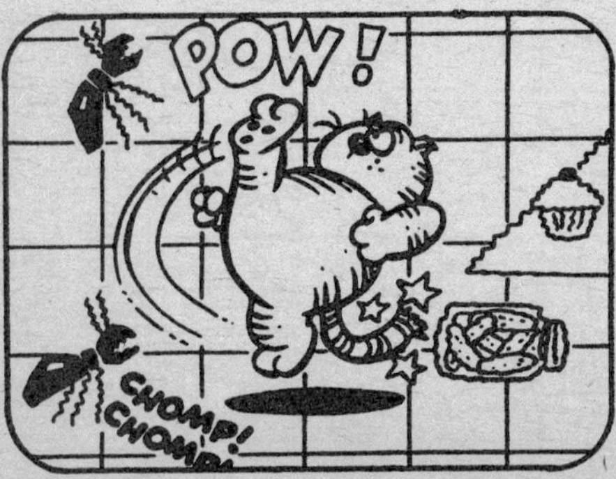
POW!
CHOMP!
CHOMP

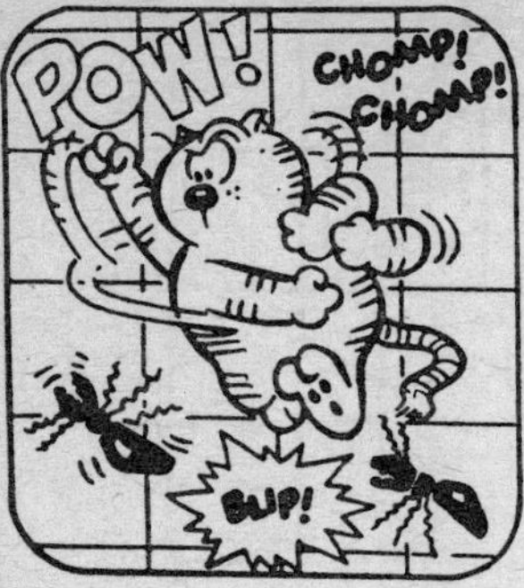
POW!
CHOMP!
CHOMP!
BLIP!

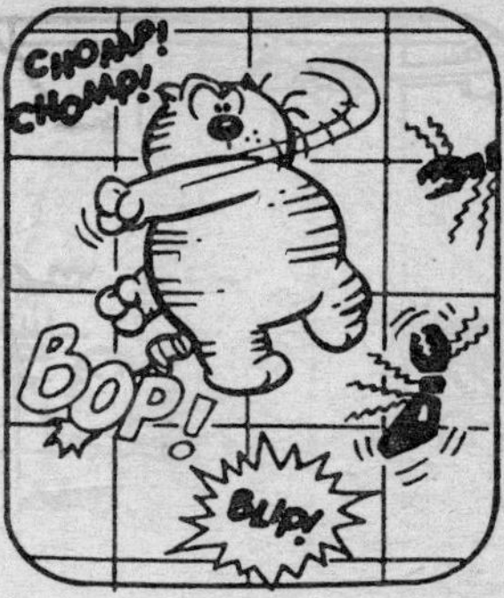
CHOMP!
CHOMP!
BOP!
BLIP!

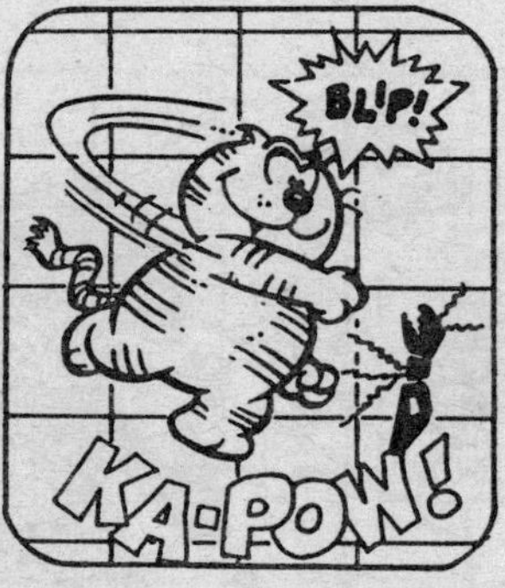
BLIP!
KA-POW!

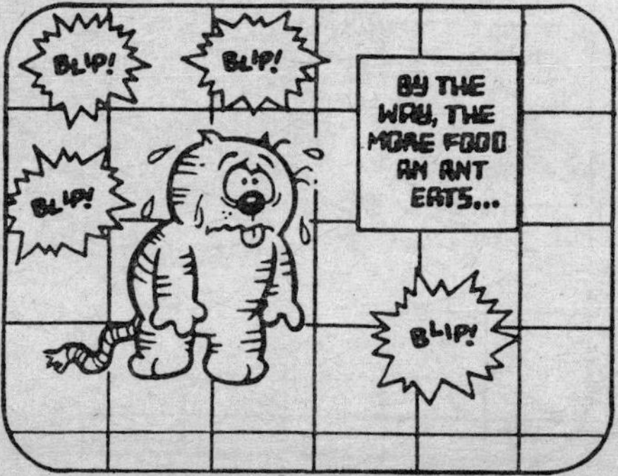
BLIP!
BLIP!
BLIP!
BY THE WAY, THE MORE FOOD AN ANT EATS...
BLIP!

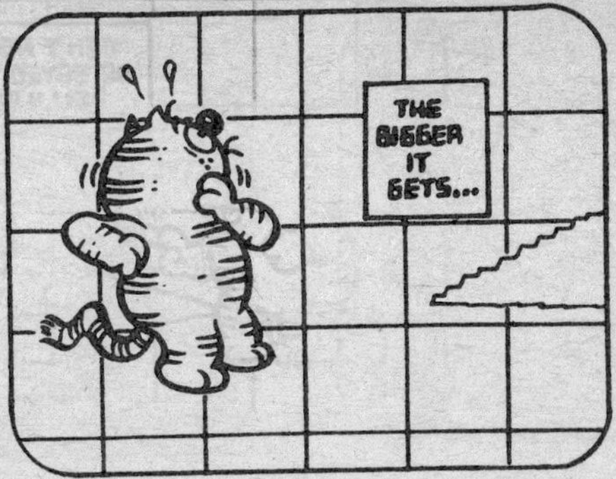
THE BIGGER IT GETS...

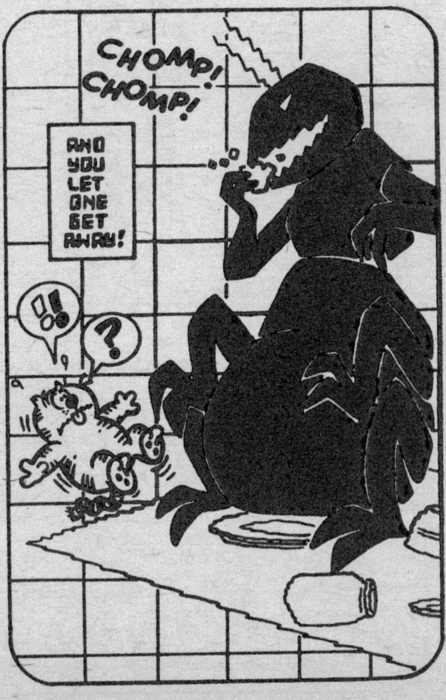
CHOMP! CHOMP!
AND YOU LET ONE GET AWAY!
!!
?

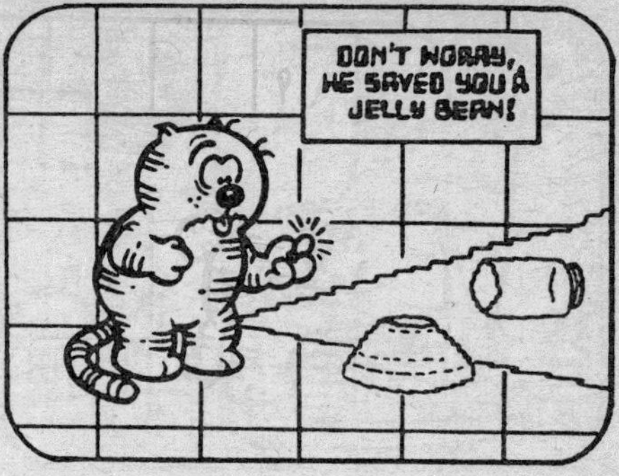
DON'T WORRY, HE SAVED YOU A JELLY BEAN!

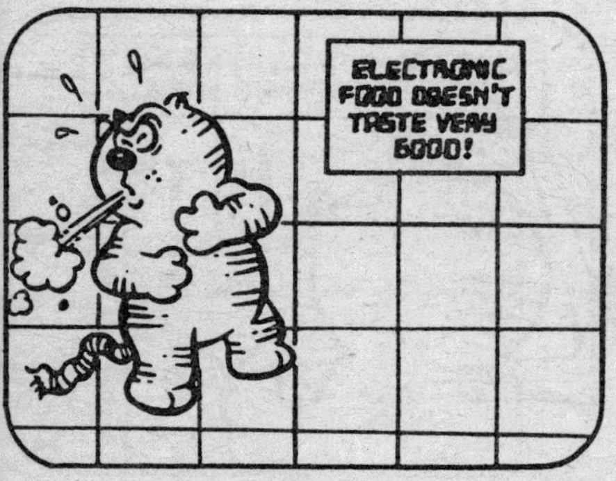
ELECTRONIC FOOD DOESN'T TASTE VERY GOOD!

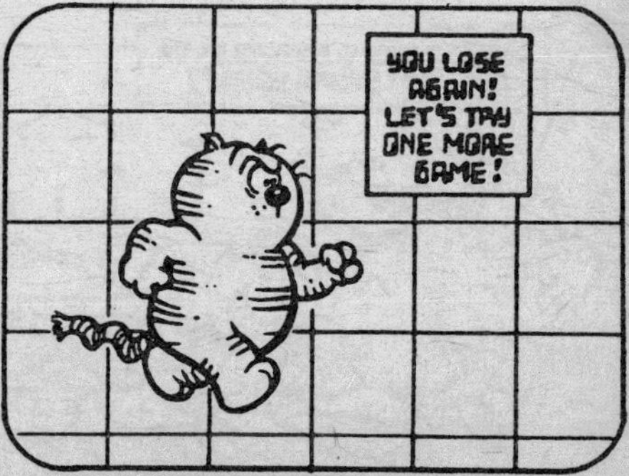
YOU LOSE AGAIN! LET'S TRY ONE MORE GAME!

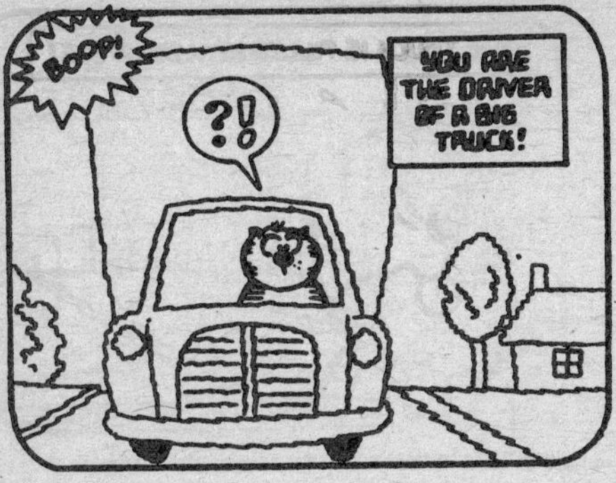
BOOP!
?!
YOU ARE THE DRIVER OF A BIG TRUCK!

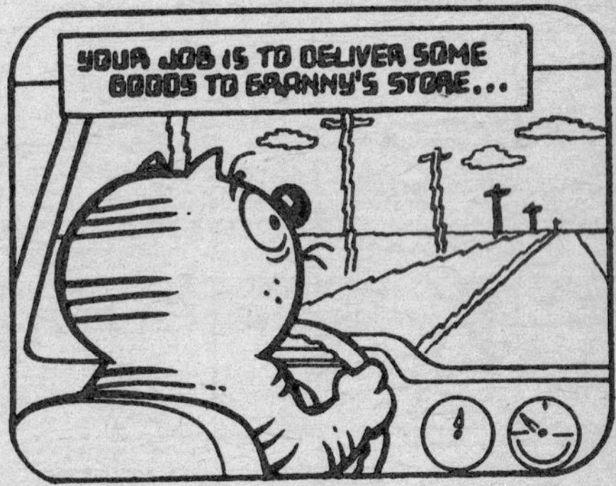
YOUR JOB IS TO DELIVER SOME GOODS TO GRANNY'S STORE...

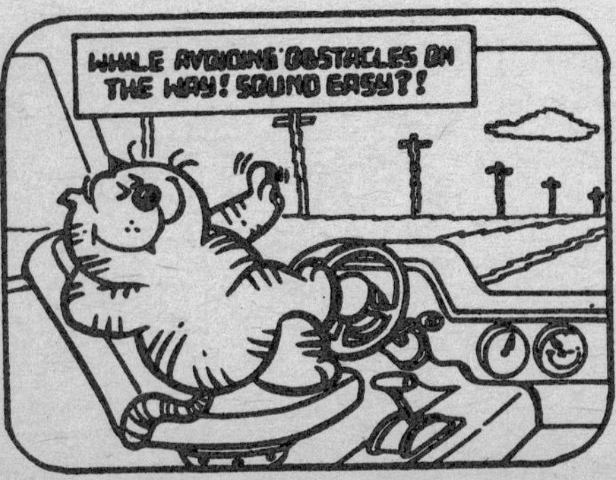
WHILE AVOIDING OBSTACLES ON THE WAY! SOUND EASY?!

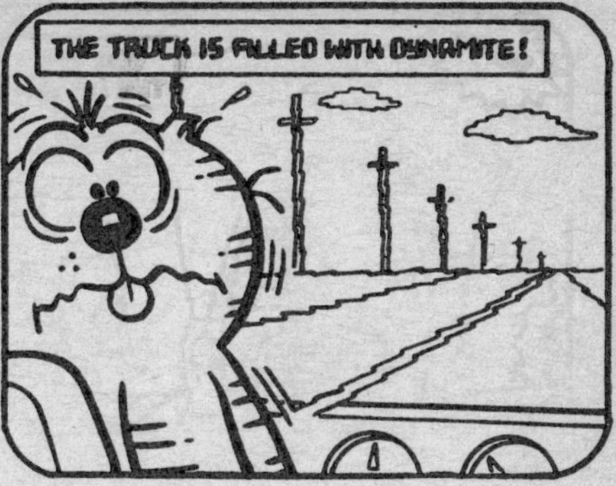
THE TRUCK IS FILLED WITH DYNAMITE!

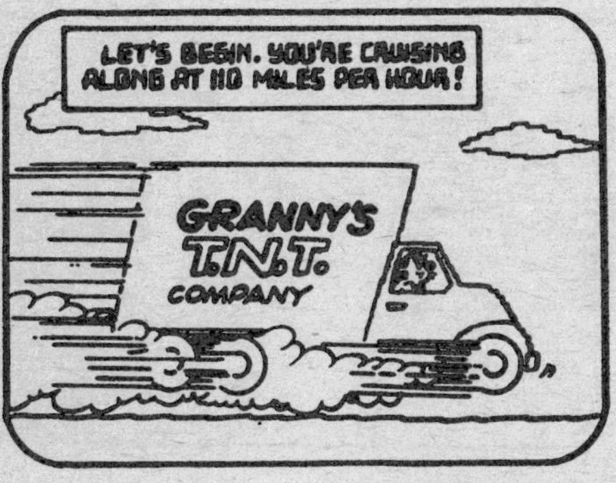
LET'S BEGIN. YOU'RE CRUISING ALONG AT 110 MILES PER HOUR!
GRANNY'S T.N.T. COMPANY

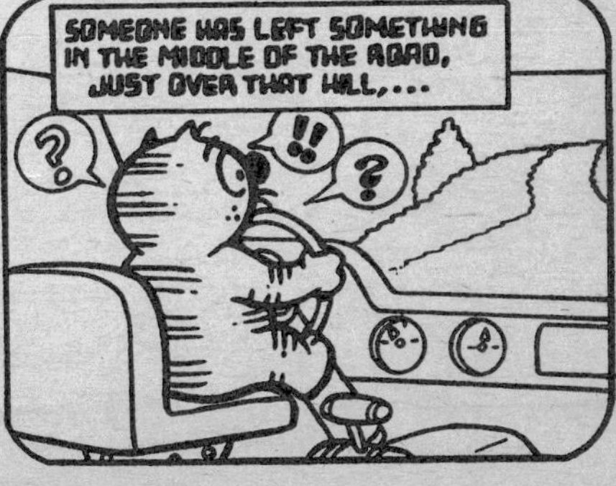
SOMEONE HAS LEFT SOMETHING IN THE MIDDLE OF THE ROAD, JUST OVER THAT HILL,...
?
!!
?

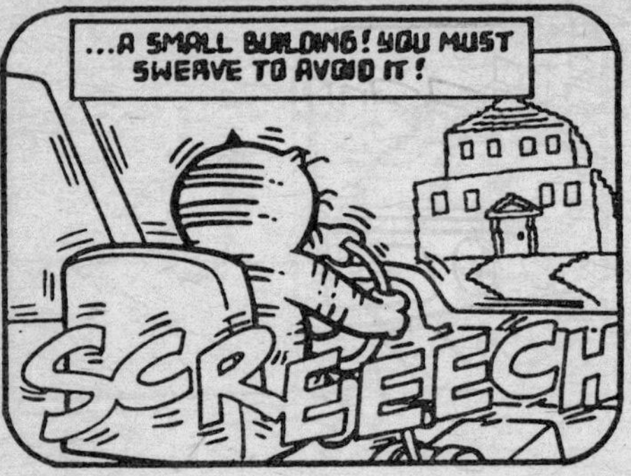
...A SMALL BUILDING! YOU MUST SWEAVE TO AVOID IT!
SCREEECH

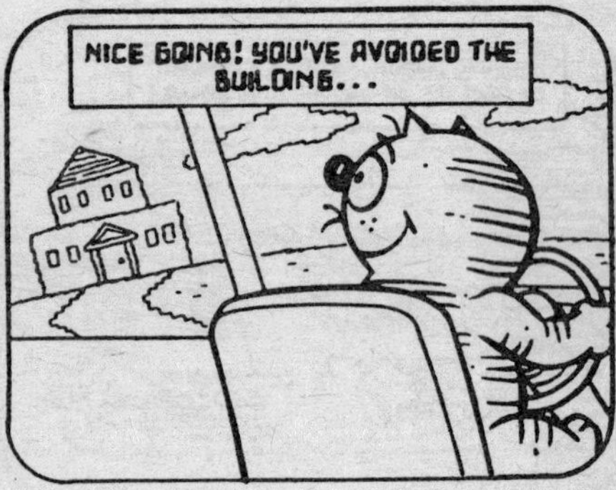
NICE GOING! YOU'VE AVOIDED THE BUILDING...

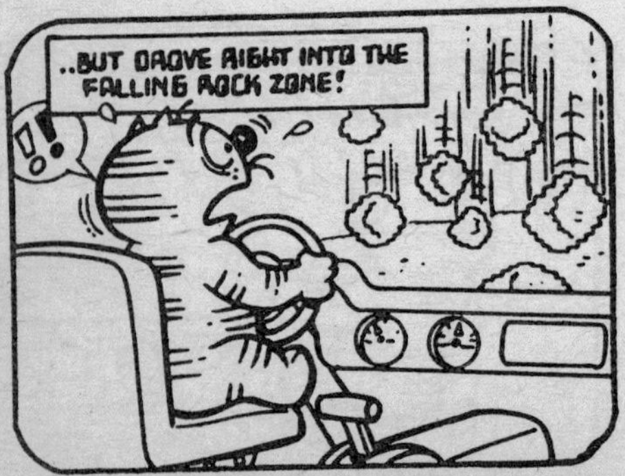
..BUT DROVE RIGHT INTO THE FALLING ROCK ZONE!

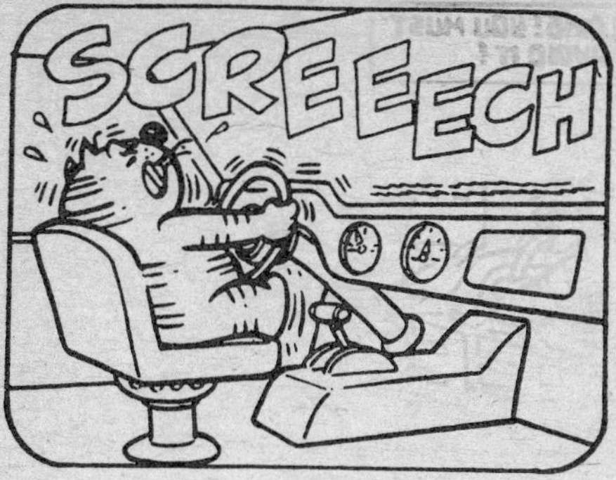
SCREEECH

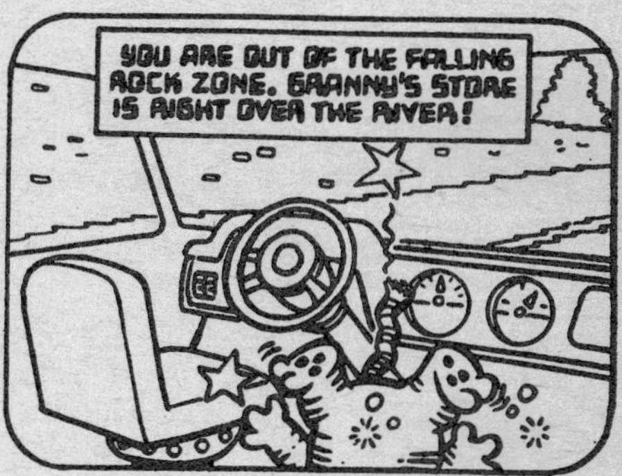
YOU ARE OUT OF THE FALLING ROCK ZONE. GRANNY'S STORE IS RIGHT OVER THE RIVER!

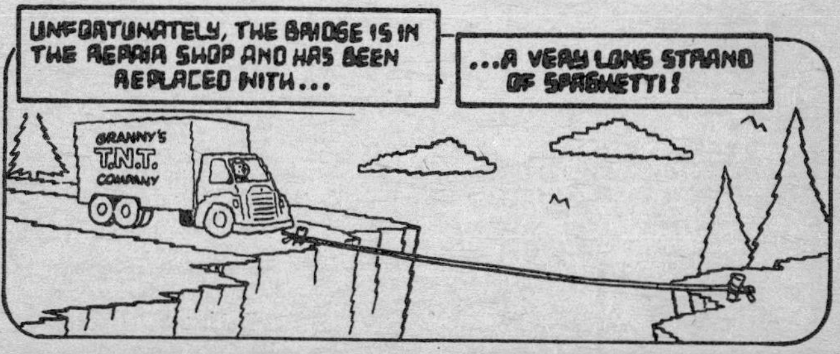
UNFORTUNATELY, THE BRIDGE IS IN THE REPAIR SHOP AND HAS BEEN REPLACED WITH...
...A VERY LONG STRAND OF SPAGHETTI!
GRANNY'S T.N.T. COMPANY

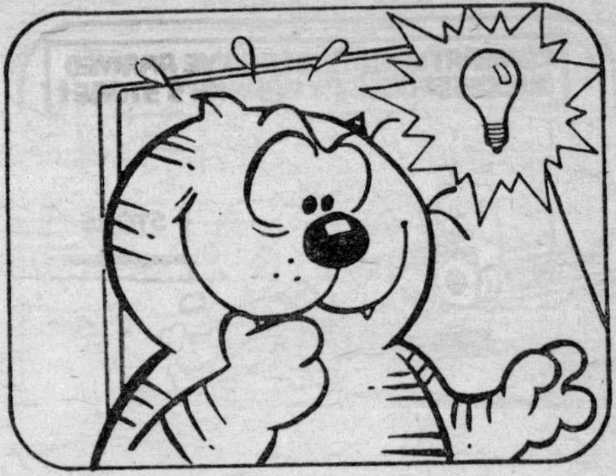

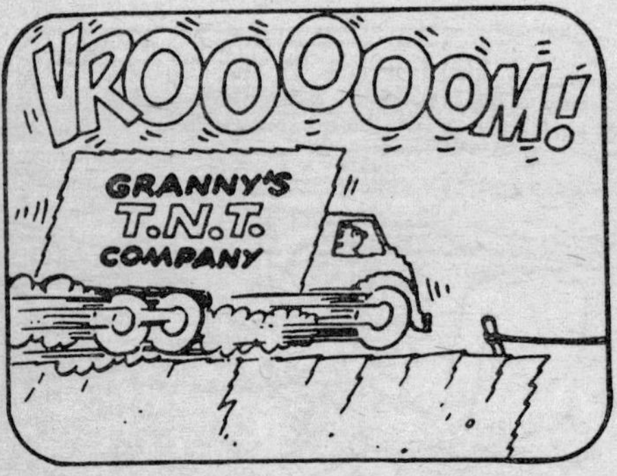
VROOOOOM!
GRANNY'S
T.N.T.
COMPANY

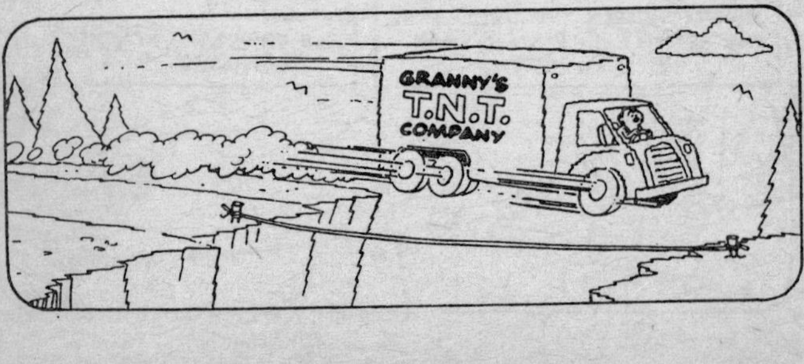
GRANNY'S
T.N.T.
COMPANY

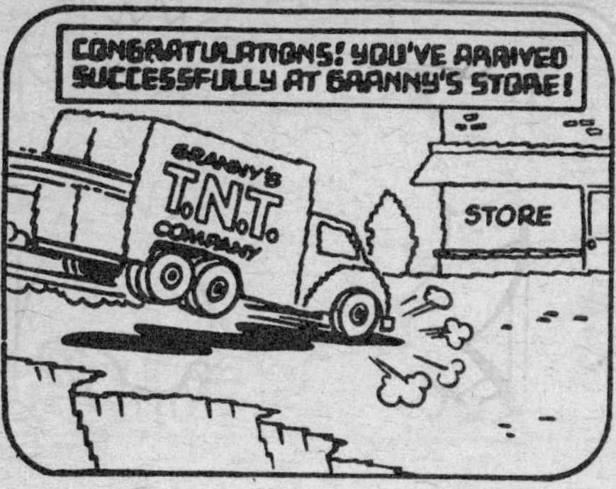
CONGRATULATIONS! YOU'VE ARRIVED SUCCESSFULLY AT GRANNY'S STORE!
GRANNY'S T.N.T. COMPANY
STORE

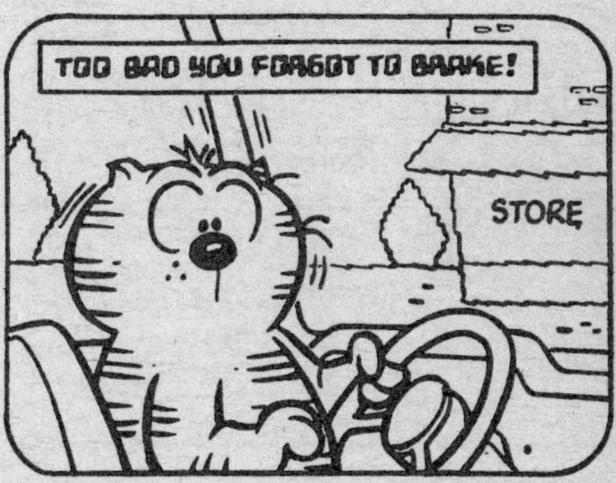
TOO BAD YOU FORGOT TO BRAKE!
STORE

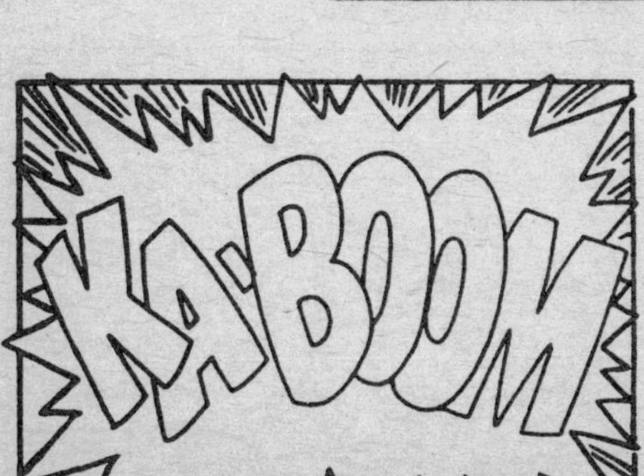
KA-BOOM

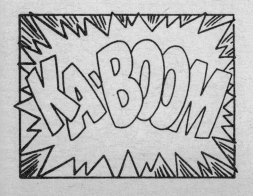

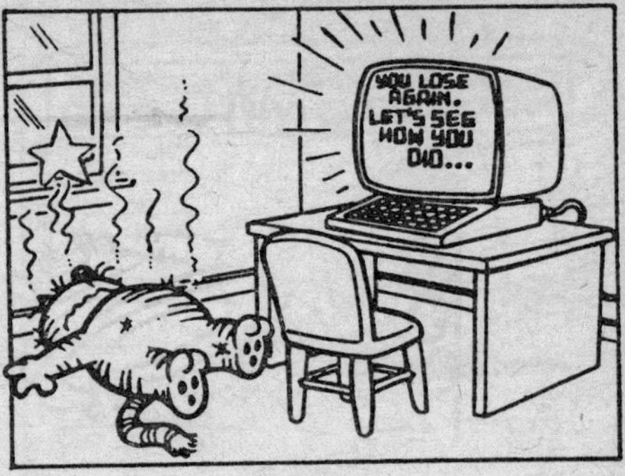
YOU LOSE AGAIN. LET'S SEE HOW YOU DID...

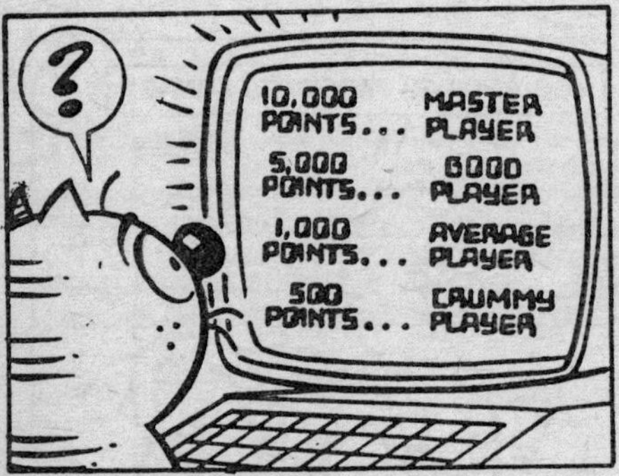
?
10,000 POINTS... MASTER PLAYER
5,000 POINTS... GOOD PLAYER
1,000 POINTS... AVERAGE PLAYER
500 POINTS... CRUMMY PLAYER

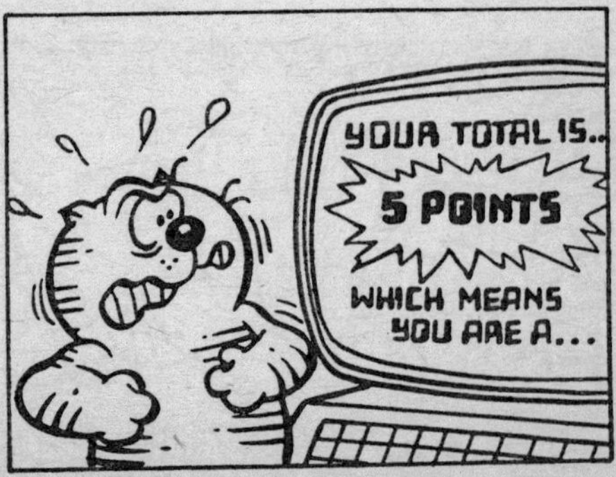
YOUR TOTAL IS...
5 POINTS
WHICH MEANS YOU ARE A...

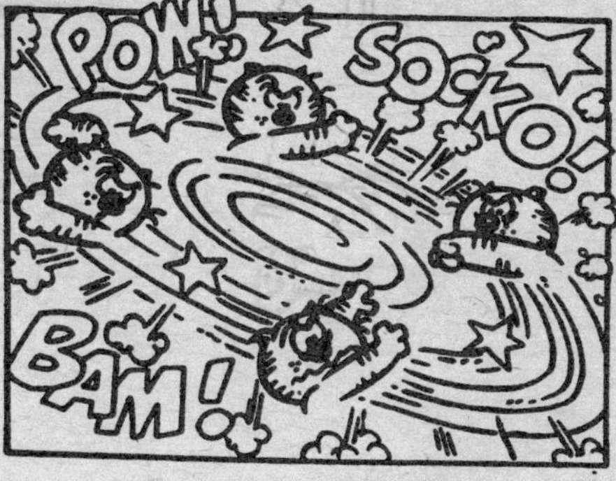
POW!
SOCKO!
BAM!

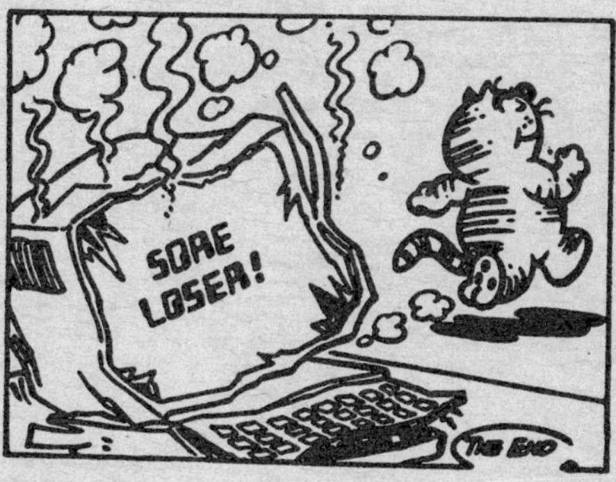
SORE LOSER!
THE END

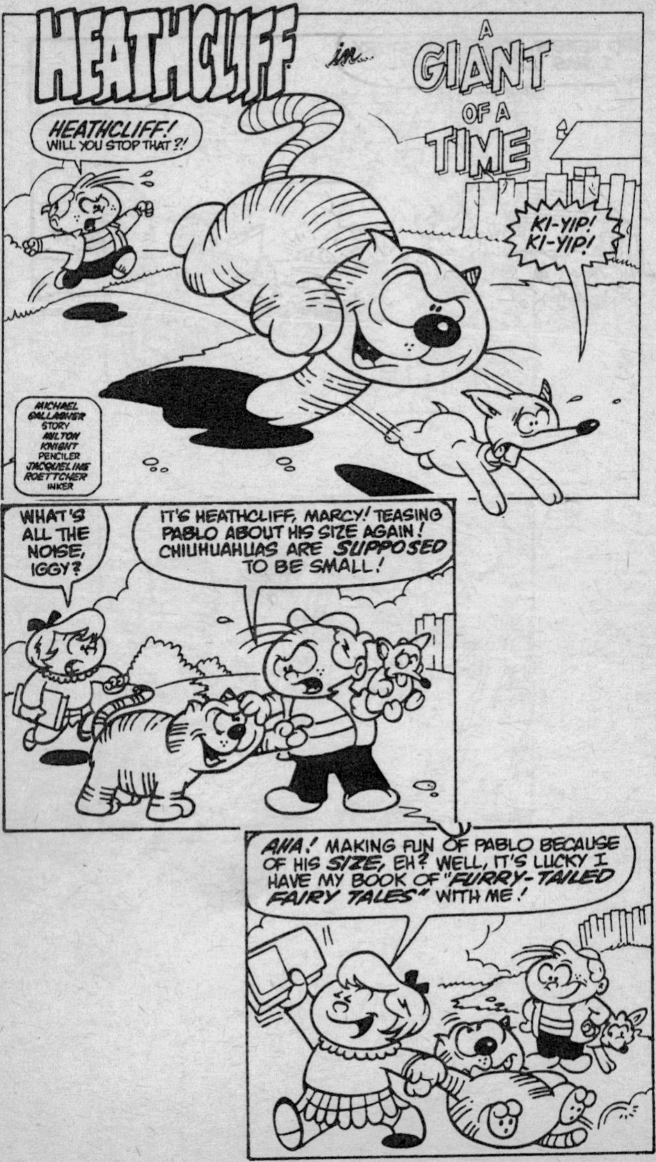
HEATHCLIFF
in...
A GIANT OF A TIME
HEATHCLIFF! WILL YOU STOP THAT?!
KI-YIP! KI-YIP!
MICHAEL GALLAGHER STORY
MILTON KNIGHT PENCILER
JACQUELINE ROETTCHER INKER
WHAT'S ALL THE NOISE, IGGY?
IT'S HEATHCLIFF, MARCY! TEASING PABLO ABOUT HIS SIZE AGAIN! CHIHUAHUAS ARE SUPPOSED TO BE SMALL!
AHA! MAKING FUN OF PABLO BECAUSE OF HIS SIZE, EH? WELL, IT'S LUCKY I HAVE MY BOOK OF "FURRY-TAILED FAIRY TALES" WITH ME!

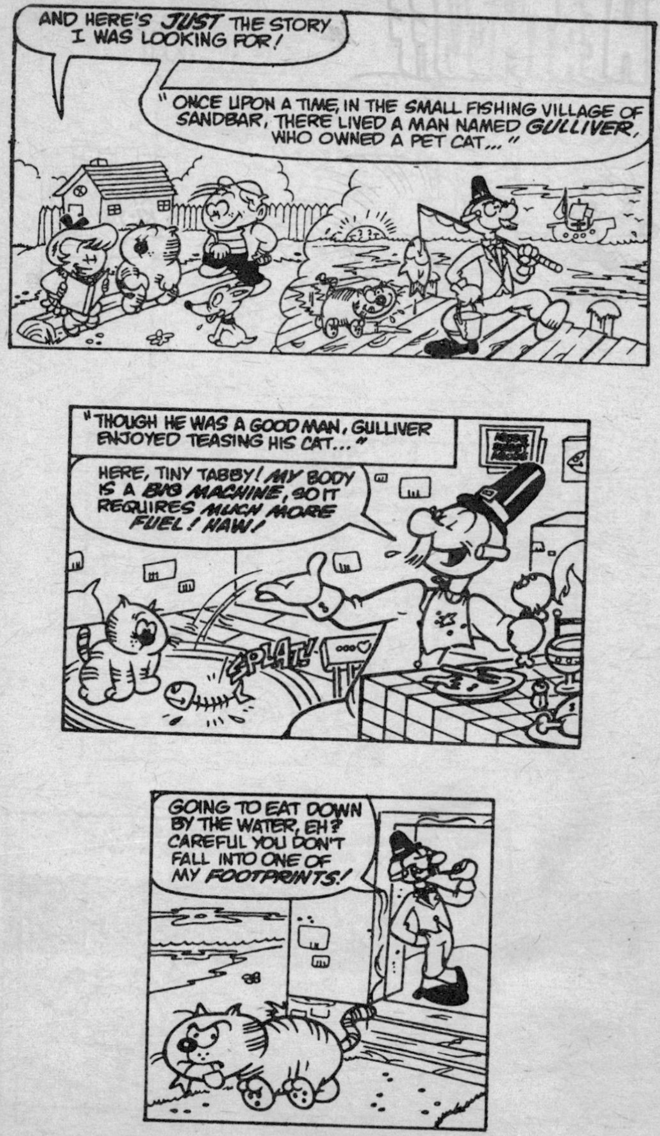
AND HERE'S JUST THE STORY I WAS LOOKING FOR!
"ONCE UPON A TIME, IN THE SMALL FISHING VILLAGE OF SANDBAR, THERE LIVED A MAN NAMED GULLIVER, WHO OWNED A PET CAT..."
"THOUGH HE WAS A GOOD MAN, GULLIVER ENJOYED TEASING HIS CAT..."
HERE, TINY TABBY! MY BODY IS A BIG MACHINE, SO IT REQUIRES MUCH MORE FUEL! HAW!
SPLAT!
GOING TO EAT DOWN BY THE WATER, EH? CAREFUL YOU DON'T FALL INTO ONE OF MY FOOTPRINTS!

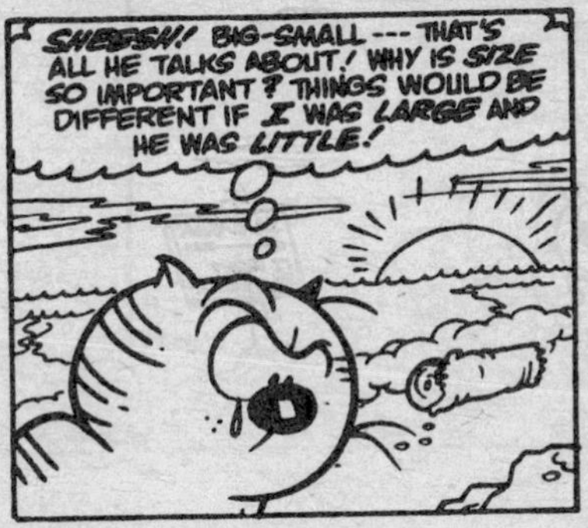
SHEESH! BIG-SMALL --- THAT'S ALL HE TALKS ABOUT! WHY IS SIZE SO IMPORTANT? THINGS WOULD BE DIFFERENT IF I WAS LARGE AND HE WAS LITTLE!

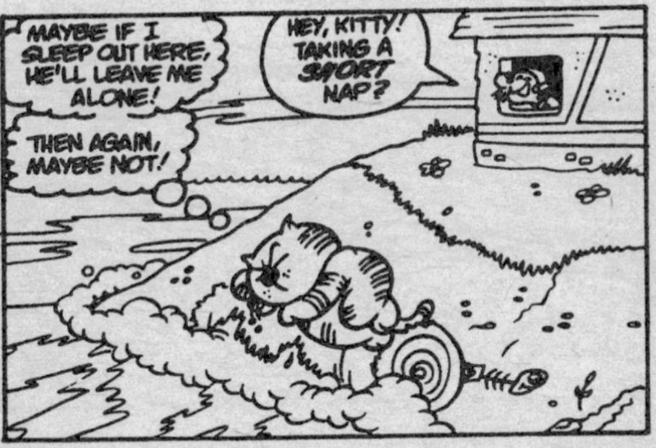
MAYBE IF I SLEEP OUT HERE, HE'LL LEAVE ME ALONE!
HEY, KITTY! TAKING A SHORT NAP?
THEN AGAIN, MAYBE NOT!

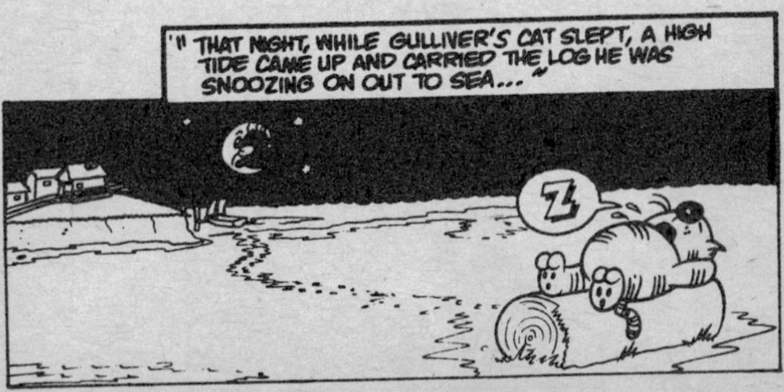
"THAT NIGHT, WHILE GULLIVER'S CAT SLEPT, A HIGH TIDE CAME UP AND CARRIED THE LOG HE WAS SNOOZING ON OUT TO SEA..."
Z

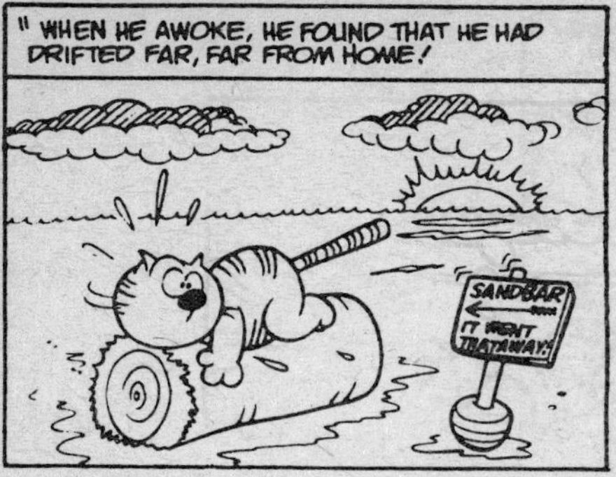
"WHEN HE AWOKE, HE FOUND THAT HE HAD DRIFTED FAR, FAR FROM HOME!
SANDBAR
IT WENT THATAWAY!

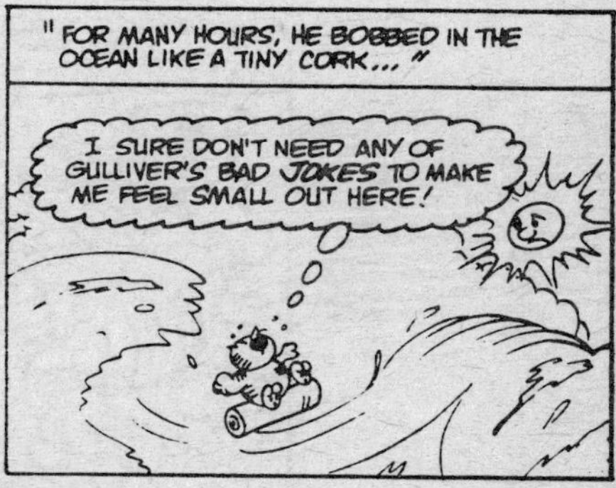
"FOR MANY HOURS, HE BOBBED IN THE OCEAN LIKE A TINY CORK..."
I SURE DON'T NEED ANY OF GULLIVER'S BAD JOKES TO MAKE ME FEEL SMALL OUT HERE!

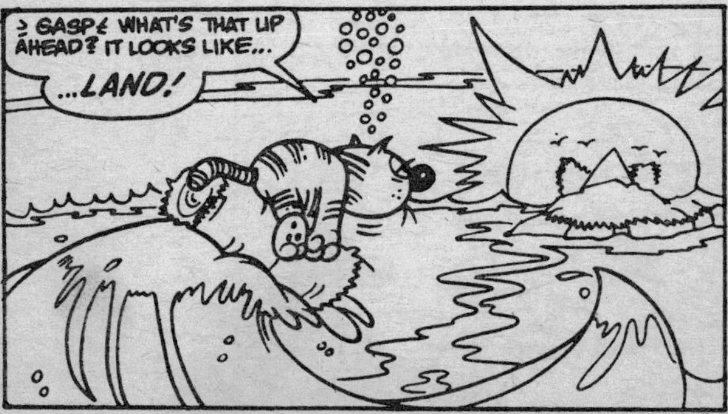
≥GASP≤ WHAT'S THAT UP AHEAD? IT LOOKS LIKE...
...LAND!

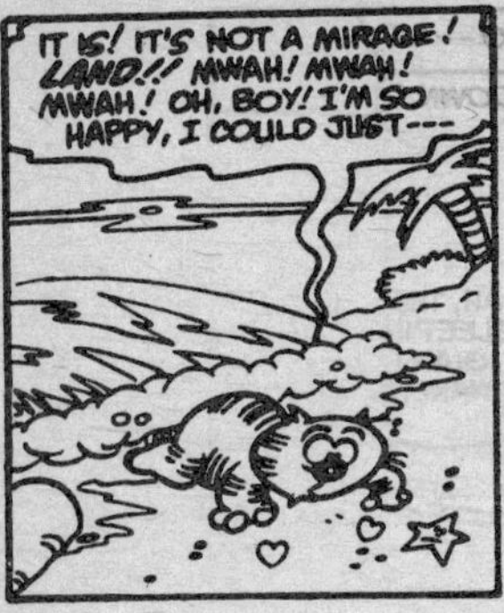
IT IS! IT'S NOT A MIRAGE! LAND!!! MWAH! MWAH! MWAH! OH, BOY! I'M SO HAPPY, I COULD JUST---

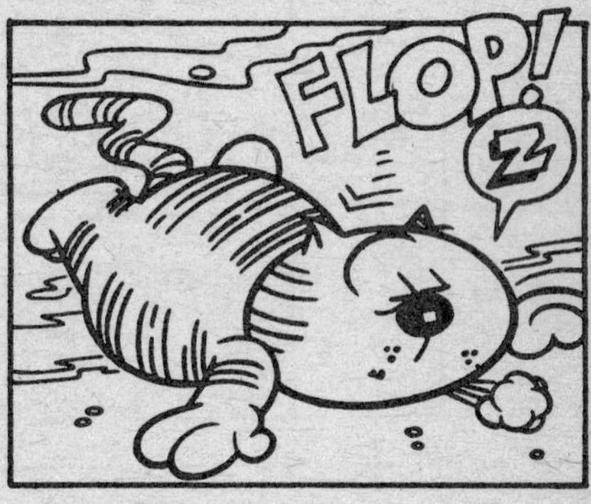
FLOP!
Z

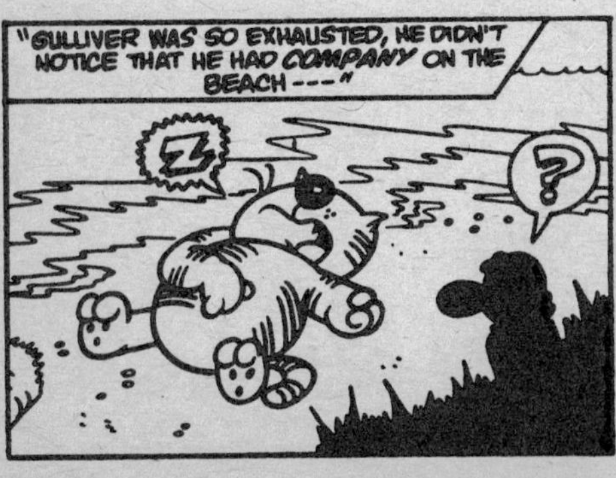
"GULLIVER WAS SO EXHAUSTED, HE DIDN'T NOTICE THAT HE HAD COMPANY ON THE BEACH---"
Z
?

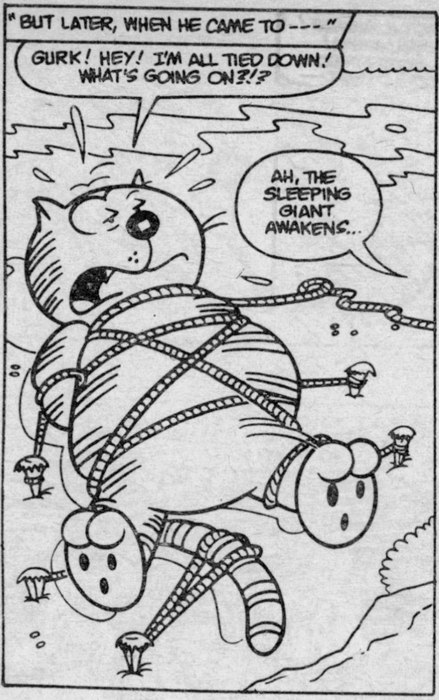
"BUT LATER, WHEN HE CAME TO---"
GURK! HEY! I'M ALL TIED DOWN! WHAT'S GOING ON?!?
AH, THE SLEEPING GIANT AWAKENS...

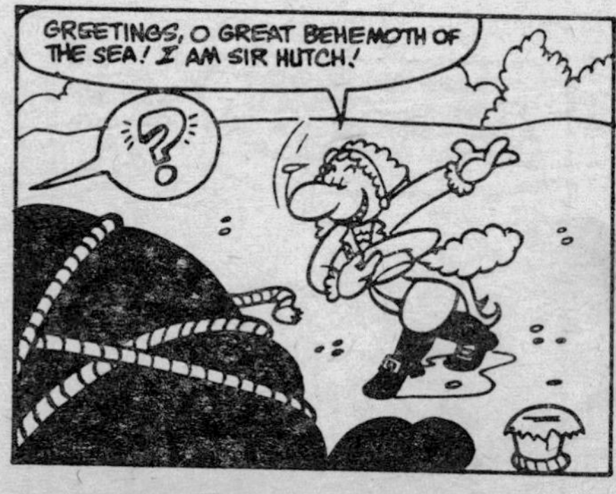
GREETINGS, O GREAT BEHEMOTH OF THE SEA! I AM SIR HUTCH!
?

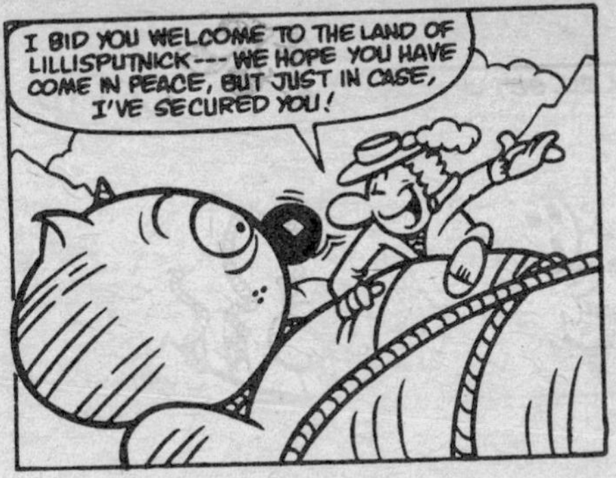
I BID YOU WELCOME TO THE LAND OF LILLISPUTNICK--- WE HOPE YOU HAVE COME IN PEACE, BUT JUST IN CASE, I'VE SECURED YOU!

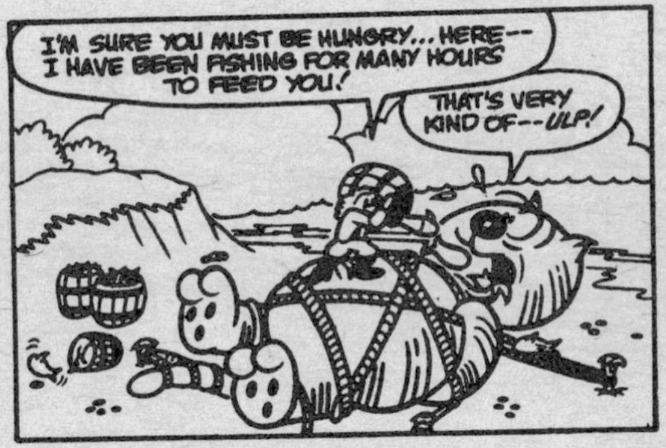
I'M SURE YOU MUST BE HUNGRY... HERE-- I HAVE BEEN FISHING FOR MANY HOURS TO FEED YOU!
THAT'S VERY KIND OF--ULP!

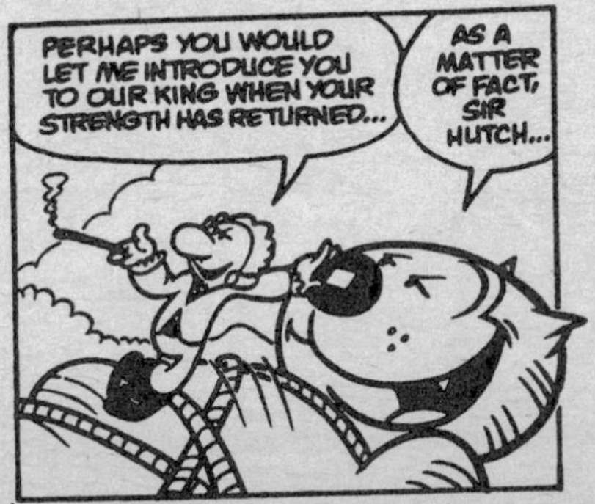
PERHAPS YOU WOULD LET ME INTRODUCE YOU TO OUR KING WHEN YOUR STRENGTH HAS RETURNED...
AS A MATTER OF FACT, SIR HUTCH...

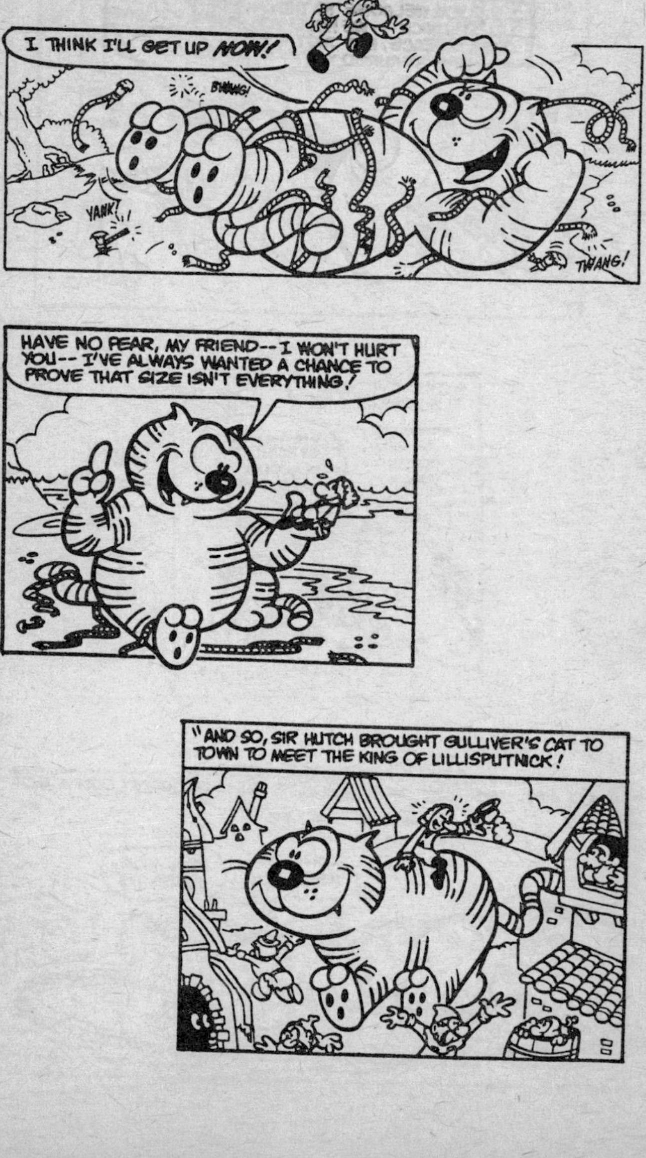
I THINK I'LL GET UP NOW!
BWANG!
YANK!
TWANG!
HAVE NO FEAR, MY FRIEND-- I WON'T HURT YOU-- I'VE ALWAYS WANTED A CHANCE TO PROVE THAT SIZE ISN'T EVERYTHING!
"AND SO, SIR HUTCH BROUGHT GULLIVER'S CAT TO TOWN TO MEET THE KING OF LILLISPUTNICK!

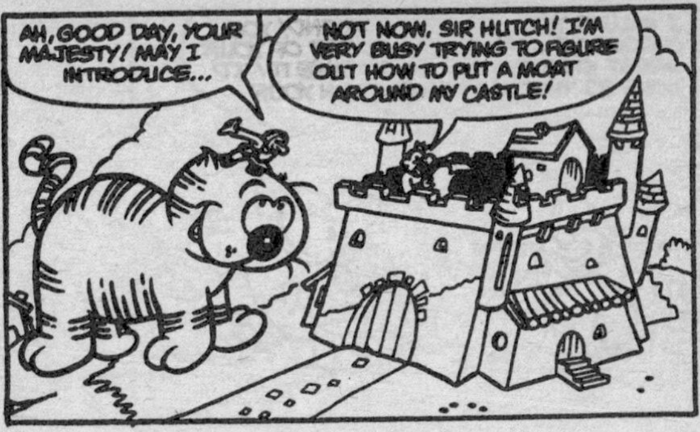
AH, GOOD DAY, YOUR MAJESTY! MAY I INTRODUCE...
NOT NOW, SIR HUTCH! I'M VERY BUSY TRYING TO FIGURE OUT HOW TO PUT A MOAT AROUND MY CASTLE!

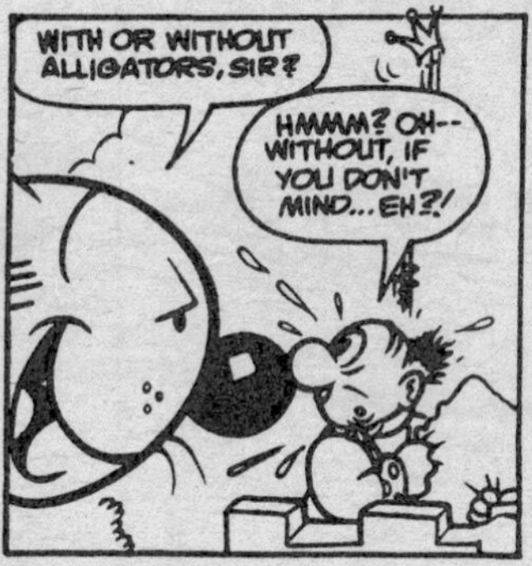
WITH OR WITHOUT ALLIGATORS, SIR?
HMMM? OH-- WITHOUT, IF YOU DON'T MIND... EH?!

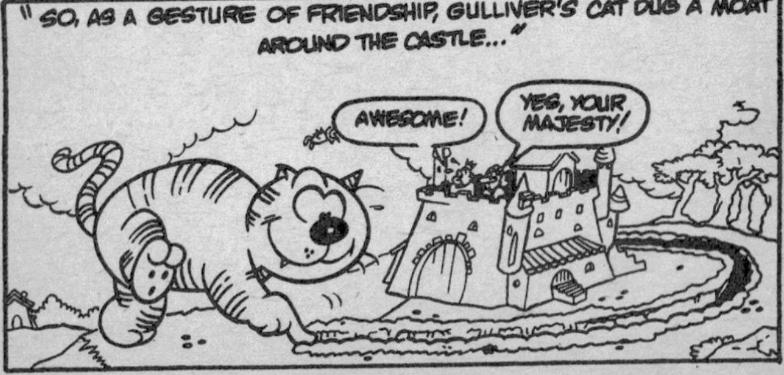
"SO, AS A GESTURE OF FRIENDSHIP, GULLIVER'S CAT DUG A MOAT AROUND THE CASTLE..."
AWESOME!
YES, YOUR MAJESTY!

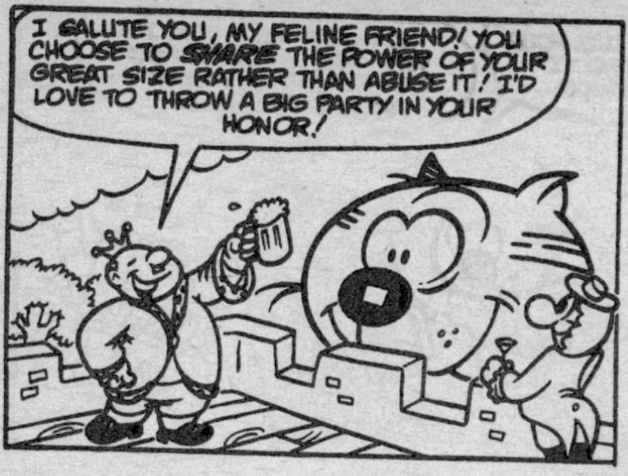
I SALUTE YOU, MY FELINE FRIEND! YOU CHOOSE TO SHARE THE POWER OF YOUR GREAT SIZE RATHER THAN ABUSE IT! I'D LOVE TO THROW A BIG PARTY IN YOUR HONOR!

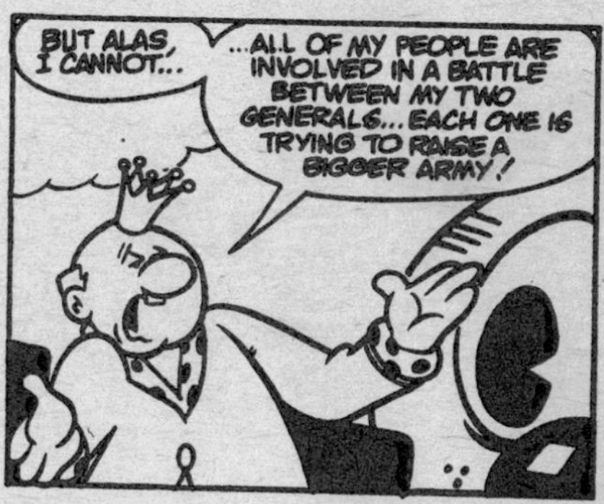
BUT ALAS, I CANNOT...
...ALL OF MY PEOPLE ARE INVOLVED IN A BATTLE BETWEEN MY TWO GENERALS... EACH ONE IS TRYING TO RAISE A BIGGER ARMY!

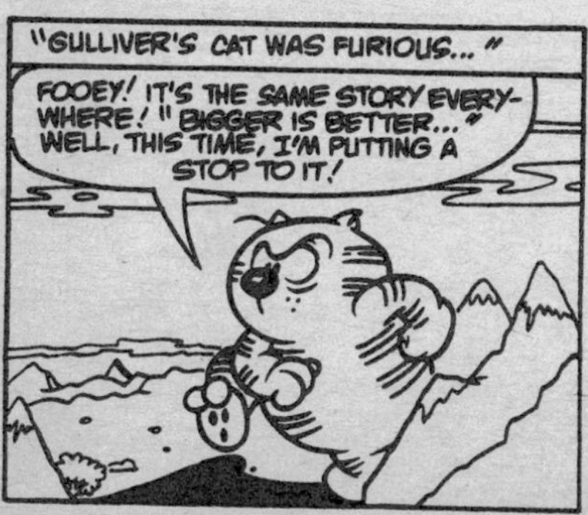
"GULLIVER'S CAT WAS FURIOUS..."
FOOEY! IT'S THE SAME STORY EVERY-WHERE! "BIGGER IS BETTER..." WELL, THIS TIME, I'M PUTTING A STOP TO IT!

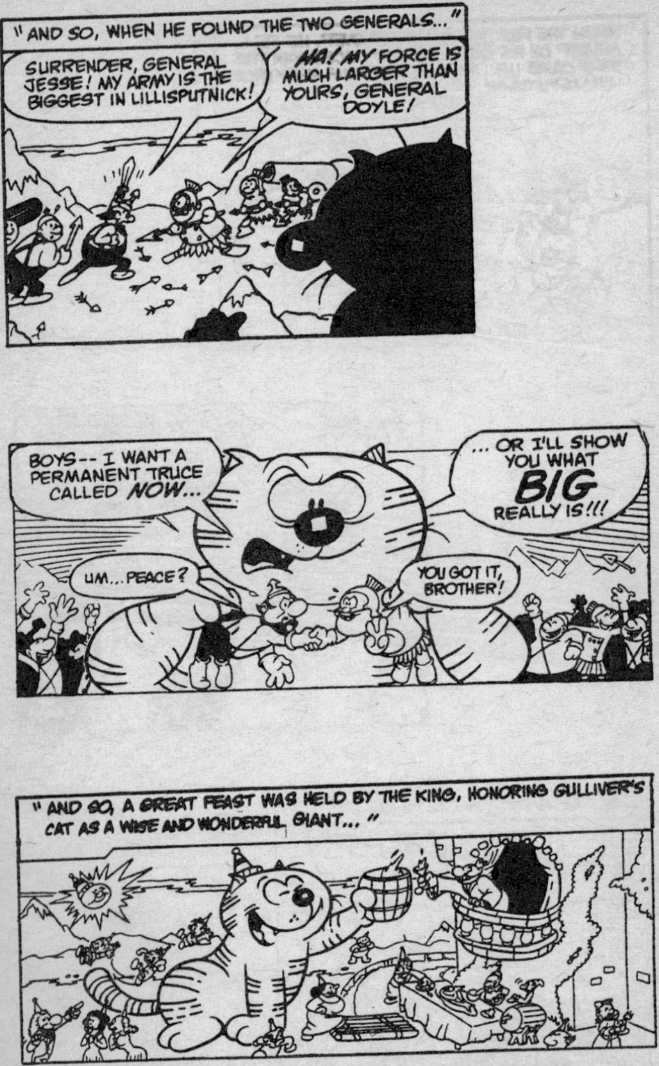
"AND SO, WHEN HE FOUND THE TWO GENERALS..."
SURRENDER, GENERAL JESSE! MY ARMY IS THE BIGGEST IN LILLISPUTNICK!
HA! MY FORCE IS MUCH LARGER THAN YOURS, GENERAL DOYLE!
BOYS-- I WANT A PERMANENT TRUCE CALLED NOW...
... OR I'LL SHOW YOU WHAT BIG REALLY IS!!!
UM... PEACE?
YOU GOT IT, BROTHER!
"AND SO, A GREAT FEAST WAS HELD BY THE KING, HONORING GULLIVER'S CAT AS A WISE AND WONDERFUL GIANT..."

" WHEN THE FESTIVITIES WERE OVER, HE FELL ASLEEP ON HIS OLD LOG. AND ONCE AGAIN THE TIDE CAME UP... AND CARRIED HIM AWAY FROM LILLISPUTNICK. "

Z

" WHEN HE WOKE UP, HE WAS BACK IN HIS HOME TOWN OF SANDBAR! "

"AND BACK WITH GULLIVER, WHO WAS OVERJOYED TO SEE HIS CAT--- "

I'M SO GLAD YOU CAME HOME, KITTY! FROM NOW ON, NO MORE JOKES ABOUT YOUR SIZE! FROM NOW ON, LET'S JUST LIVE HAPPILY EVER AFTER!

"WHICH IS JUST WHAT THEY DID!"

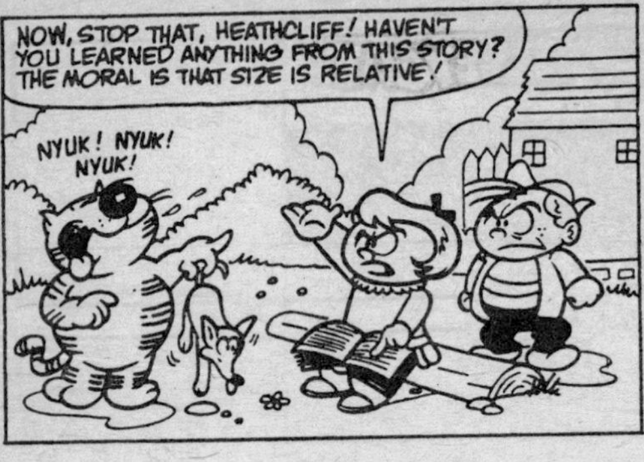
NOW, STOP THAT, HEATHCLIFF! HAVEN'T YOU LEARNED ANYTHING FROM THIS STORY? THE MORAL IS THAT SIZE IS RELATIVE!
NYUK! NYUK! NYUK!

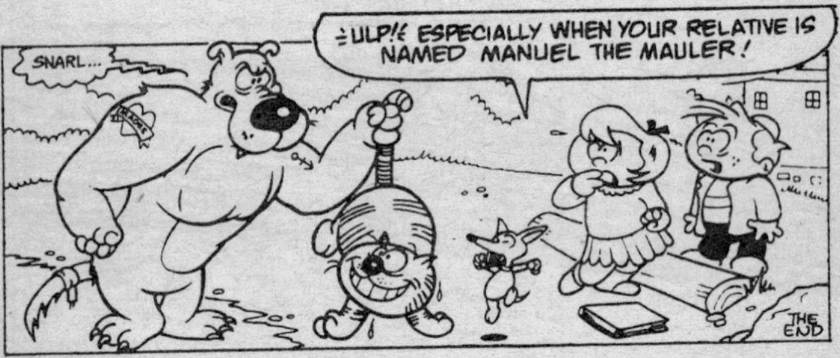
SNARL...
ULP! ESPECIALLY WHEN YOUR RELATIVE IS NAMED MANUEL THE MAULER!
THE END

HEATHCLIFF in "ALLEYCAT"
!
KA-BLANG!
SLURP! SLURP!
SLURP!
MILK
MILK
END

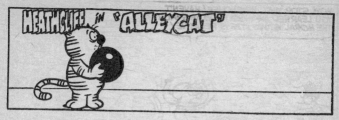

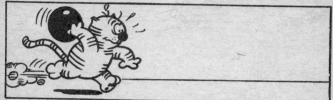

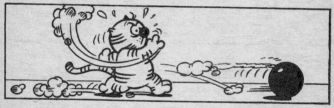

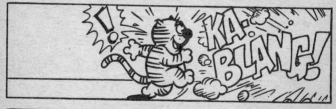

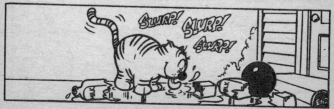

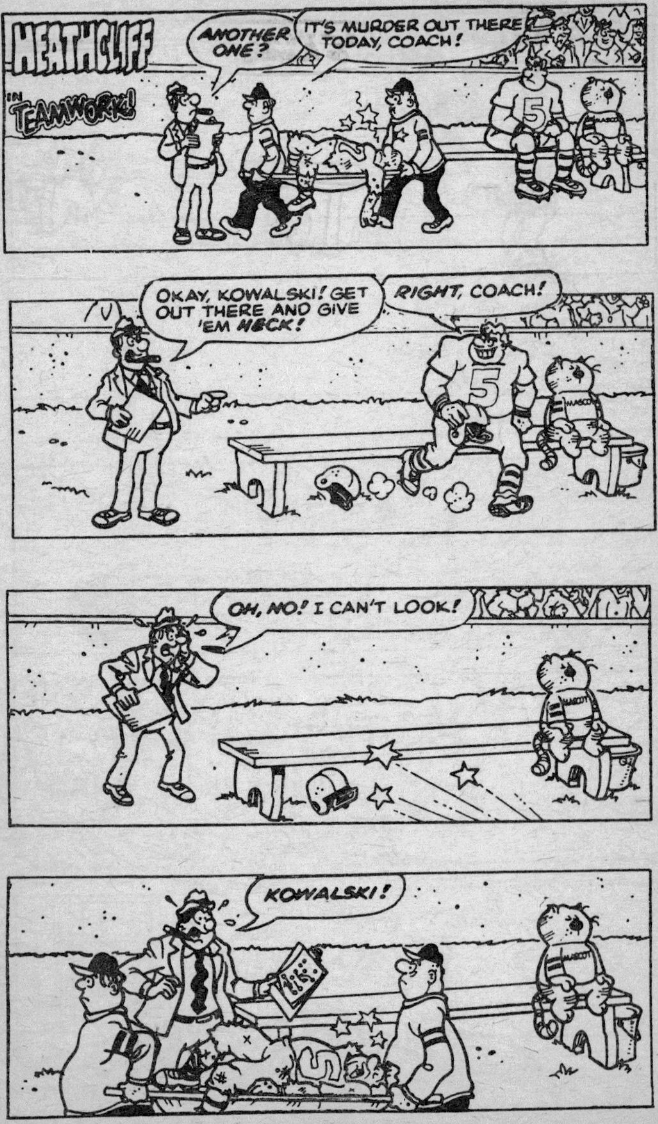
HEATHCLIFF
IN TEAMWORK!
ANOTHER ONE?
IT'S MURDER OUT THERE TODAY, COACH!
5
MASCOT
OKAY, KOWALSKI! GET OUT THERE AND GIVE 'EM HECK!
RIGHT, COACH!
OH, NO! I CAN'T LOOK!
KOWALSKI!

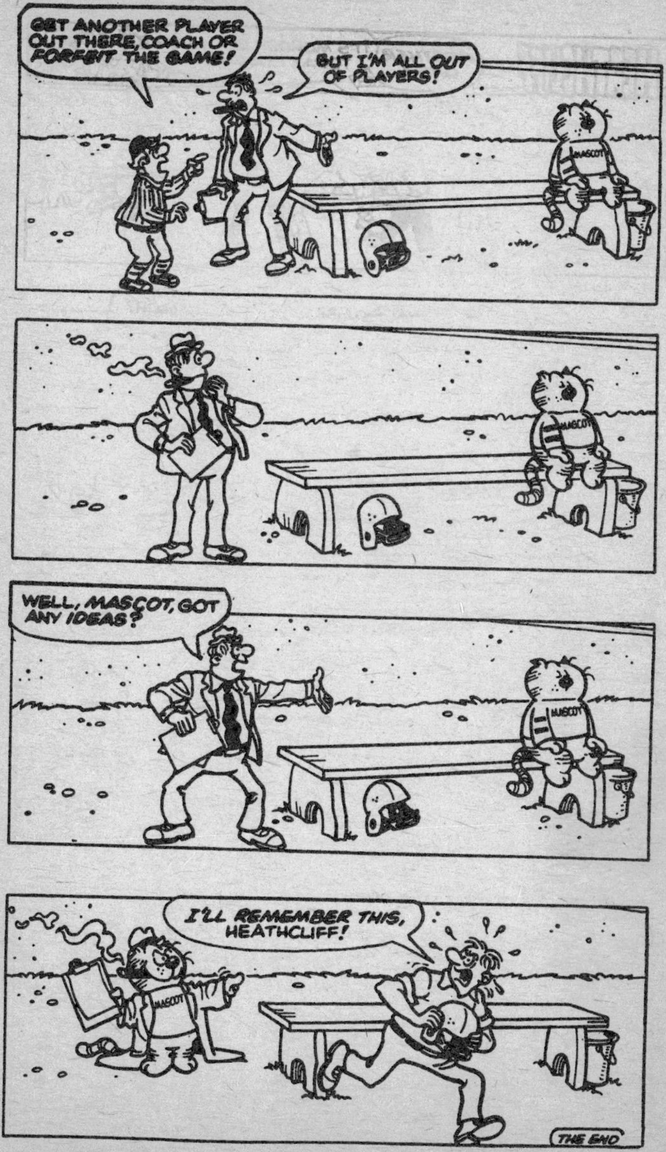
GET ANOTHER PLAYER OUT THERE, COACH OR FORFEIT THE GAME!
BUT I'M ALL OUT OF PLAYERS!
MASCOT
MASCOT
WELL, MASCOT, GOT ANY IDEAS?
MASCOT
MASCOT
I'LL REMEMBER THIS, HEATHCLIFF!
THE END